INFANT ASSEMBLIES

Sheila Davidson

Scripture Union

130 City Road, London EC1V 2NJ

First published 1983
Reprinted 1985
Revised edition 1986
Reprinted 1988

ISBN 0 86201 137 X

Printed at The Bath Press, Avon

CONTENTS

INTRODUCTION

This Assembly material for Infant school children is intended to meet the need of teachers who want to use outlines which are both soundly child related and teach positive Christian truths.

The outlines are set out according to themes rather than weeks and they may be spread over more Assemblies than suggested in the book.

The children should be encouraged to follow up ideas in their own classrooms and to bring back contributions to future Assemblies.

Families

INTRODUCTION

The joy of living in a family; how we can help one another. Suggest the children make books about their family, perhaps using pictures from catalogues. Make class graphs showing how many people in the family. Ask children to find out who is the tallest, shortest etc.

1ST DAY   MY DAD

Children could show paintings and pictures about their fathers; describe what they look like, activities in which they take part and how fathers show they love their families. Briefly discuss ways of helping Daddy at home.

Prayer   Thank you, God, for our Dads; for the way they care for us, the work they do for us and the games they play with us. Please help us to make them glad by being helpful and cheerful at home. Amen.

Song   'Praise him'. *Come and Sing*, Scripture Union

2ND DAY   THE PRODIGAL SON: A STORY ABOUT A FATHER

Bible story   Luke chapter 15, verses 11–24
Aim to stress the great love that the father in the story had for his son.

The loving father

Once there was a farmer who was very kind and loving. He had a big farm with animals and plants growing for food. He had two boys who helped him on the farm. They helped to look after the animals and the crops. They always had enough food to eat and plenty of clothes to wear. Their father took good care of them both, and loved them very much. When the boys grew up one of them, the older one, still liked to help his father but the other one, the younger boy, got a bit tired of working and he thought, 'I don't want to stay on this farm any more. One day my father will share out all his money between me and my brother

11

and we'll have half of the farm each; but I don't want to wait all that time until my father is an old, old man; I want my share *now*.' So he went to his good kind father and said, 'I want my share of your money *now*.' His father was sad but he shared out his money, some for one boy, some for the other. The younger one was very pleased and he said, 'Father, I'm leaving the farm. I want to go away and see other parts of our country. I want adventures.' So off he went with his share of the money. He found a big town and he had a lovely time. He bought new clothes and delicious food and he went to lots of parties where he made new friends. He forgot all about his father, but his father didn't forget about him. Soon his money began to run out; he had only three coins left, then two, then one, then none. The people who were his friends didn't want to be friends any more and he had no money left to buy food. His clothes began to wear out. He still forgot about his father, but his good kind father didn't forget about him. The boy decided he would have to get a job, so he went to a man and said, 'Could I look after your pigs?' The man let him do this. The pigs had food to eat, but the boy had nothing. *Then* the boy suddenly remembered his good kind father at home. 'At home I always had enough food. I have been very silly; I shall go home and ask my father if I can work again on his farm. I don't expect he'll let me be like his own boy again, but he might let me stay on the farm and look after the animals.' So he started off home. Now every day his good kind father had been looking out for his boy and when he was still a long way from the farm his father saw him coming back home and he didn't feel cross at all. He ran down the road to meet his boy and hugged him. The boy said, 'Father, I have been very silly. I don't think you'll want me to be your son, your child, any more.' But his father said, 'I love you. I'm so glad to have you home.' He found new clothes for his boy and a lovely ring to wear on his finger. Then he arranged a special party, because he was so pleased to see him. His father said, 'I was sad while you were away, but now I am glad you are home.' That is a story that Jesus told his friends and he said, 'God is just like that good kind father in the story.'

Prayer   Thank you, God, that you are a loving Father. Thank you that you always love us and are caring for us all the time. Amen.

Song   'God is a Father'. *Come and Sing*, Scripture Union.
OR   'I'm very glad of God'. *Someone's Singing, Lord*, A & C Black.
OR   'God takes good care of me'. *Come and Sing*.

12

3RD DAY   MY MUM

Children could show paintings and pictures about their mothers; maybe a class book called 'How Mummy helps me'. Discuss ways of helping Mum at home.

Prayer   Thank you, God, for my Mummy. Thank you for the cooking and sewing and washing she does for me. Thank you for the way she comforts me when I am sad and tucks me up in bed at night. Amen.
Song   'Hands to work'. *Someone's Singing, Lord*, A & C Black.
OR   'I can't see the wind'. *Come and Sing*, Scripture Union.

4TH DAY   HANNAH AND SAMUEL: A STORY ABOUT A MOTHER

Bible story   1 Samuel chapter 1
Aim to show how mothers look forward to having children and caring for them; how God knew Hannah was sad and gave her the gift of a baby. This story can be found in 'The Very Special Present', *Young People of the Bible* series, Lutterworth Publishing House.

Prayer   Thank you, God, for giving Hannah a baby. Thank you for listening to me when I talk to you. Amen.
Song   'God who made the earth'. *Sing to God*, Scripture Union.

5TH DAY   MY GRANDPARENTS

Who is a grandmother? – mother of Daddy or Mummy. Who is a grandfather? – father of Daddy or Mummy. Let children say what they specially like doing with grannies and grandads – going for tea, staying the night, having special treats, how grannies often knit them jumpers and grandads tell them stories about when they were little boys. Discuss how we can help older people.

Prayer   Thank you, God, for grannies and grandads. Thank you for the stories they tell us and the things they make for us. Thank you that they have time to listen to us. Please help us to think of ways of making them happy too. Amen.
Song   'Hands to work'. *Someone's Singing, Lord*. A & C Black.

6TH DAY   RUTH AND NAOMI: A STORY ABOUT A GRANDMOTHER

Bible story   Ruth chapters 1, 2 and 4: 13–17
Aim to show how Ruth brought joy to Naomi by her kindness and unselfishness.
The story can be found in *Storytime 2*, page 17, Scripture Union.

Prayer   Thank you God for all the kind things that Ruth did for Naomi. Please help us to think of ways of making life happier and easier for older people. Amen.

Song   'Jesus' hands were kind hands'. *Someone's Singing Lord*. A & C Black

7TH DAY   BROTHERS AND SISTERS

Most families have several children; discuss the sizes of families. How many children are there in your house? Older brothers and sisters often help younger ones. Do you sometimes quarrel? Jesus wants us to love our brothers and sisters and share things with them.
An appropriate story is *Big sister and little sister*, by Charlotte Zolotow, a Piccolo picture book, Pan Books Ltd.

Prayer   Thank you, God, for our brothers and sisters and the fun we have with them. Help us to play well together without fighting. Help us to share our toys and not always want the first turn in a game. Amen.

Song   'God whose name is Love'. *Hymns and Songs*, Ladybird Books.

OR   'Be kind'. *Come and Sing*, Scripture Union.

8TH DAY   BLESSING THE CHILDREN

Bible story   Matthew chapter 19, verses 13–15
This story can be found in *Storytime 1*, page 79, Scripture Union.
Aim to stress the fun of going out for the day to see Jesus, the sadness when they were turned away and finally the joy when Jesus called them back.

Prayer Thank you, Lord Jesus, that you are never too busy or too tired to love me. Thank you because you love all children everywhere. Amen.

Song 'Jesus is the best friend'. *Come and Sing*, Scripture Union.

9TH DAY   BABIES

Discuss the joy of having a new baby in the house. What sort of things does a baby do? What sort of things does a baby need? – (bottle, pram, playpen etc) What can we do to help look after our baby brothers or sisters? – (rock the pram, hand things to Mummy when she is bathing the baby, play quietly when the baby is asleep etc) What things do babies learn to do? – (sit up, crawl, walk, talk etc)
An appropriate book might be *The New Baby* by Althea, Dinosaur Publications.

Prayer Thank you, God, for our baby brothers and sisters and all the joy they bring us. We love to see them smile and touch us with their tiny fingers. May we help our parents to look after them and always be gentle and loving. Amen.

Song 'Be kind'. *Come and Sing*, Scripture Union.

10TH DAY   MOSES IN THE BULRUSHES:
A STORY ABOUT A BABY

Bible story   Exodus chapter 2, verses 1–10
This story may be found in *Storytime 2*, page 5, Scripture Union.
Aim to bring out the family's joy when the baby arrived, their sadness when the king wanted no baby boys in his land, their excitement planning to hide the baby; how the princess found him and asked Moses' mother to bring him up for her. Show how wonderfully God looked after that family.

Prayer Thank you, God, for taking care of baby Moses. Please help my Mummy and Daddy to take care of me. Amen.

Song 'God takes good care of me'. *Come and Sing*, Scripture Union.

OR 'Loving Father of all children'. *Come and Sing*, Scripture Union.

Prayers on page 28 of *The Lion Book of Children's Prayers*, Lion Publishing, are about families and could be used where appropriate.

Our useful bodies

1ST DAY   HANDS

Hold out your hands – what do we use our hands for? Let children give ideas – holding, folding, tying, writing, carrying, swinging etc. Let a group of children show something they have made with their hands; perhaps a painting, clay model or sewing. Children could show pictures made with hand prints and suggest others might like to try. Our hands are very useful – who can we help? Suggest ways such as clearing away toys, putting spoons on the table for tea etc.

Prayer   Thank you, God, for my useful hands. Please make me quick to see ways of using them to help other people. Amen.

Song   'Hands to work'. *Someone's Singing, Lord*, A & C Black.

2ND DAY   THE MAN WITH THE BAD HAND

Bible story   Luke chapter 6, verses 6–11
This story can be found in *Bible Storytime*, Book 3, Story 15, International Bible Reading Association.
Aim to show that Jesus always knows when people are sad and cares very much about them.

Prayer   Dear Lord Jesus, thank you for caring about the man with a bad hand. Thank you for caring about me. Amen.

Song   'Jesus' hands were kind hands'. *Someone's Singing, Lord*, A & C Black.

3RD DAY   FEET

The children could show footprints made by stepping into paint and then walking across paper. Ask one child to take off shoes and socks and look at different parts of the leg and foot; knee, shin, ankle, toes, sole, heel. Our feet are useful, what can they do? Encourage children to answer – run, climb, kick a ball, paddle etc. How can we use our feet to be helpful? – going somewhere with a message, running upstairs to fetch something Granny has forgotten etc.

Prayer   Thank you, God, for our strong, useful legs and feet. May we use them to help other people. Amen.

Song   'For all the strength we have'. *Someone's Singing, Lord*, A & C Black.

4TH DAY   THE MAN BY THE POOL

Bible story   John chapter 5, verses 2–9
This story may be found in *Storytime 2*, page 49, Scripture Union.
Aim to show that Jesus knew the man could not walk and also knew he was lonely and needed a friend to help him.

Prayer   Thank you, Jesus, that you were a friend to the lonely man who could not walk. Thank you for wanting to be my friend too and that you will help me every day. Amen.

Song   'Jesus is the best Friend'. *Come and Sing*, Scripture Union.

5TH DAY   EYES

Have something beautiful for the children to look at – flowers, piece of material, a picture. Ask the children to think of times when their eyes are very useful – for finding the toy or game they need, for recognising the person they want to talk with, for reading and looking at pictures, for crossing the road etc. If we could not see what would we have to do? (feel) Play a feeling game; blindfold some children and give them objects to identify eg brush, soap, a plastic beaker. Remind the children how fortunate we are to be able to see the things around us.

Prayer   Thank you, God, for our eyes and the beautiful things you have made which we can see and enjoy. Help us to look out for ways of helping other people. Amen.

Song   'Hands to work' (specially notice 2nd verse, 'Eyes to see'). *Someone's Singing, Lord*, A & C Black.
Useful books: *Touching*, Think About Books, Franklin Watts.
Sally can't see, Palle Peterson, A & C Black.

6TH DAY THE HEALING OF A BLIND MAN

Bible story Mark chapter 10, vs 46–52, and Luke chapter 18, vs 35–43
This story is told in *Jesus heals a Blind Man*, 'Talkabouts' series, published by The Bible Societies. And also in *Storytime 1*, page 62, Scripture Union. It would be appropriate to introduce the story with an explanation of what the word blind means and maybe end the Assembly with a discussion about how we help blind people in our country today.
Aim of the story: to show that Jesus always listens to us when we ask for help.

Prayer Thank you, Lord Jesus, for making the blind man better. We pray today for all blind people. May they know how much you love them. Amen.
Song 'Jesus' hands were kind hands'. *Someone's Singing, Lord*, A & C Black.

7TH DAY EARS

Play a game with the children. Beforehand record sounds on a tape recorder. Play them one by one to the children and ask them to guess what made the noise, eg kettle boiling, electric mixer, cleaning teeth, striking match, winding clock etc. What did we use to hear these sounds?

How our ears are useful
What do we like to hear with our ears? (Voices of our friends, traffic, birds singing, television)
Suggest children might like to make a book about sounds they like to hear.

Prayer Thank you, God, for my ears and for the many sounds I hear, especially for the voices of my family and friends and for stories being read to me. Amen.
Song 'Hands to work' (2nd verse – 'ears to hear'). *Someone's Singing, Lord*, A & C Black.
Useful books: *Tasting, Smelling*, Think About Books, Franklin Watts.

8TH DAY   THE HEALING OF THE DEAF AND DUMB MAN

Bible story   Mark chapter 7, verses 31–37
This story can be found in *Storytime 1*, page 54, Scripture Union.
Before the story the word 'deaf' will need to be explained and the children helped to understand how lonely a deaf person must feel. It will also be necessary to explain why deaf people are often unable to talk clearly, as we learn to talk by listening to others speaking.

Prayer   Thank you, Lord Jesus, for healing the deaf man. We know that deaf children sometimes feel lonely. Please help them to know how much you love them. Amen.
Song   'For all the strength we have'. *Someone's Singing, Lord*, A & C Black.
Useful books: *I can't hear like you, I can't talk like you*, Althea, Dinosaur Publications.

9TH DAY   SMELL AND TASTE

Have a selection of things for the children to smell and ask them to guess what they are, eg coffee, lavender, peppermint. The children would need to be blindfolded. Similarly have a selection of things to taste, eg salt, sugar, apple, chocolate. Suggest children look at their tongue in a mirror at home and see the tiny sensitive lumps which help us to taste.
Discuss the importance of being able to smell and taste, eg smell when something is burning or taste when food is bad. Ask the children what sort of things they like to taste and smell.

Prayer   Part of a prayer from *The Lion Book of Children's Prayers*, Lion Publishing, page 62, beginning 'For sausages, baked beans and chips'. Use the first four lines only.
OR   Dear God, I am glad I can taste crunchy apples and smooth chocolate. I am glad I can smell the scent of flowers and toast being made for breakfast. Thank you for all your gifts to me. Amen.
Song   'Praise him'. *Come and Sing*, Scripture Union.
Useful books: *Tasting, Smelling*, Think About Books, Franklin Watts.

10TH DAY HANDICAPPED PEOPLE

Remind the children about some of the people they heard about in the stories – those who were blind, deaf, lame. Explain how we have clever doctors who can help people like that, but sometimes they are not made completely well and need to learn special skills, eg a person with no arms might learn to pick things up with his feet. Show some Braille if possible and discuss guide dogs for the blind. Show pictures of wheel chairs, vehicles with lifts etc. Explain how handicapped people, although they do not always *look* like us, have the same *feelings* of sadness, joy, fear, loneliness etc. Useful story might be *Claire and Emma* by Diane Peter, A & C Black.

Prayer   Dear Lord, we thank you that we can see and hear and speak. Please help the blind, the deaf and the dumb. We thank you that we can run and jump and play. Please help children who are in wheelchairs or have to lie in bed all day. Thank you for the kind people who take care of them. Amen.

OR   Lord Jesus, when I see handicapped people please help me to be kind. They don't like me to point at them or laugh because they look different. Please help me to make friends with them. Amen.

Song   'Be kind'. *Come and Sing*, Scripture Union.

People who look after our bodies

11TH DAY SCHOOL NURSE AND SCHOOL DOCTOR

(Some young children are very worried about seeing the school doctor so this is a good preparation beforehand.) Invite nurse and doctor to Assembly to show some of the things they use, eg stethoscope, large letters for testing eyesight etc, or if doctor is unable to come let a few children act the parts of doctor, parent and child. Explain why child needs to undress. Stress that doctor and nurse want to keep the children healthy and help parents to look after them.

Prayer   Thank you, God, for our school nurse and our school doctor. Thank you that they look after us so well. Amen.

Song   'For all the strength we have'. *Someone's Singing, Lord*, A & C Black.

12TH DAY SCHOOL DENTIST

Invite school dentist to Assembly if possible. Talk about keeping teeth healthy – plenty of milk, vegetables etc; not too many sweets. Clean teeth up and down as well as along. If dentist is unable to come – let a few children act the parts of dentist, assistant and child. Show little mirror and explain how it works. Stress that the school dentist only *looks* at teeth – won't carry out treatment – you have to go to clinic or own dentist for that. Read *Visiting the Dentist*, Althea, Dinosaur Publications.

Prayer Thank you, God, for our school dentist who helps me to keep my teeth healthy. Amen.
Song 'Thank you for the world so sweet'. *Hymns and Songs*, Ladybird Books.

13TH DAY AUDIOTRICIAN

Ask her to Assembly if possible and let her show children the equipment she uses – headphones in particular. Explain that her machine will make sounds and child has to say if she/he can hear anything.

Prayer Thank you, God, for our school audiotrician. Thank you that she is able to test our hearing. Thank you for all the sounds we can enjoy day by day. Amen.
Song 'I'm very glad of God'. *Someone's Singing, Lord*, A & C Black.

14TH DAY HOSPITALS

Sometimes things go wrong with our bodies. Our family doctor knows we need special care, so he sends us into hospital. Read *Going into Hospital*, Althea, Dinosaur Publications.
Let children tell or read their records of visits to hospital – stress the fact that the doctors and nurses make them better.

Prayer Dear God, we pray for people who are ill. May the doctors and nurses comfort and help them for Jesus' sake. Amen.
OR from *The Lion Book of Children's Prayers*, Lion Publishing, page 41, beginning – Great Father in heaven, thank you for doctors and nurses.

Song 'O Jesus we are well and strong'. *Someone's Singing, Lord*,
A & C Black.

Useful books: *Linda goes to hospital*, Barrie Wade, A & C Black. *Jimmy goes to the dentist*, Barrie Wade, Hamish Hamilton. *I use a wheelchair*, Althea, Dinosaur Publications. *Going to the doctor*, Althea, Dinosaur Publications.

The world in which we live

THE STORY OF CREATION

Bible story   Genesis chapter 1
Aim to show that God is the Creator of all that is good and beautiful. Also introduce the fact that the people he made are very special, because they can talk and they can love God and try to please him.
Useful books: *The World God made*, Arch Books
In the beginning, The Lion Story Bible No. 1, Lion Publishing.

Prayer   We praise you, God, for all the wonderful things you have made: the bright sun, the shining moon and the twinkling stars; for the wide expanse of sea and sky. We thank you for beautiful flowers and trees, for every living creature and for our families and friends. Help us to love you and obey you and take care of all the good things you have given us. Amen.

Song   'This is the day'. *Come and Sing Some More*, Scripture Union. The words could be changed to '*This is the world*'.

Water

1ST DAY   WHAT IS IT USED FOR?

Play some of Handel's Water Music (perhaps a short part on each of the first three days). One class tell all the other children ways in which we use water – they might have prepared a class book about it – water used for drinking, to wash in, swim in, for the washing machine, the radiator in the car etc. Stress how useful it is and what a wonderful gift God has given us. Suggest the children try some experiments with water during the next few days – what floats, what sinks; what happens when you leave a little water on a saucer in a warm place?
Children could read their own prayers thanking God for water.

Prayer Thank you, God, for water.
I like a cold drink of water on a hot day.
I like a warm soapy bath of water on a cold day.
I like to hear the water bubbling in the kettle and pans when my meals are nearly ready.
Thank you for water. Amen.

Song 'Praise him'. *Come and Sing*, Scripture Union.

2ND DAY   WHERE DOES WATER COME FROM?

Ask the children where water comes from (taps, pipes, reservoirs, rivers, rain). God sends the rain – let all this information come from the children if possible and fill in the parts they don't know. Ask the children to say what they enjoy about a rainy day – watching the raindrops trickle down a window pane, listening to the noise of the rain falling on a car roof, wearing wellingtons and splashing through puddles.
Read poems about the rain – 'Happiness' A A Milne, *Rhyme Time*, Hamlyn. 'Water has no taste at all', *Book of 1000 Poems*, Evans.

Prayer from *The Lion Book of Children's Prayers*, page 60, starting 'Our Father in heaven, we praise you'.

Song 'I love the sun'. *Come and Sing*, Scripture Union. Verse 4 is about the rain.

3RD DAY   STORY: THANK YOU FOR A DRINK OF WATER, Lion Publishing

Prayer Thank you, God, for sending the rain and for all the people who collect it and make it clean and who take care of the pipes, so that we can have a drink of water. Amen.

Song 'And God said'. *Come and Sing*, Scripture Union.

4TH DAY   BIBLE STORY: NOAH AND THE FLOOD

Bible story Genesis chapters 6–8
This story may be found in *Storytime 1*, page 9, Scripture Union. Aim to show God's care for his creatures. One class might act the story for the other children to see.
Part of the record 'Carnival of the Animals', Saint-Saëns, could be played (children might guess names of the creatures).

Prayer We remember today how Noah did just what you told him to do. Thank you for taking care of him and his family and all the animals. Thank you for taking care of me too. Amen.

Song 'God takes good care of me' (first two verses). *Come and Sing*, Scripture Union, *or* 'Trust and obey'. *Sing to God*, Scripture Union.

5TH DAY   THE SEA

The children could listen to part of 'Fingal's Cave', Mendelssohn, and maybe suggest what the music is about. Talk about the sea and how it is a vast quantity of salty water. Introduce vocabulary such as wide, deep, ocean, gigantic waves, little ripples. A picture of the sea would be helpful. Children could read about their experiences at the seaside; jumping over waves etc, or show their paintings and pictures. Look at some shells and other interesting things found at the seaside.

A poem could be used.

'There are big waves and little waves'. Eleanor Farjeon, *Young Puffin Book of Verse*.

Prayer Thank you, God, for the sea, for the way it looks on calm, still days shimmering in the sunlight. Thank you for the noise of the sea when the waves crash against the rocks or gently ripple up the beach. Thank you for the feel of the sea as it wets my toes. Amen.

OR second *prayer* on page 38 of *Lion Book of Children's Prayers*.

Song 'God made the shore'. *Come and Sing*,Scripture Union.

A useful record is 'Sea effects', Sound Effect Record, EMI.

6TH DAY   FISH

Have some goldfish in a tank for children to watch. Ask children to describe what they look like, how they feel and how they move. Show pictures of fish, some that live in rivers and lakes, others that live in the sea. Discuss gills, fins, scales; how fish are cold-blooded, how they lay eggs. Explain how people catch fish to eat. Older infants would be interested to hear about fishing boats and the sort of fish we catch around the English coast (cod, mackerel, herring). Have some pictures of tropical fish, so the children can see their beautiful shapes and colours.

Prayer Thank you, God, for fish, for their beautiful shapes and patterns and for the way they move so gracefully in the water. Thank you for the men who work hard to catch them for us to eat or for us to enjoy in our ponds and tanks. Amen.

Song The 4th verse of 'The Flowers that grow in the garden'. *Someone's Singing, Lord*, A & C Black (this verse is about fish).

OR 'And God said'. *Come and Sing*, Scripture Union.

OR 'Thank you for the world so sweet'. *Hymns and Songs*, Ladybird Books.

7TH DAY PEOPLE WHO WORK ON OR BY THE SEA

Ask the children to think of people who work by the sea or on the sea – fishermen, sailors, coastguards, divers, lifeboat men, people on oil rigs etc. Show pictures of some of them and explain what work they do. Explain how their work is hard and sometimes dangerous, also sometimes they have to go away for long periods and do not see their families as much as they would like.

Prayer Thank you, God, for all the people who work on or near the sea. When they feel lonely, help them to remember you are near them and may they work hard to please you. Amen.

Song 'God who made the earth'. *Sing to God*, Scripture Union

OR 'When lamps are lighted in the town'. *Someone's Singing, Lord*, A & C Black.

8TH DAY STILLING OF THE STORM

Bible story Mark chapter 4, verses 35–41
This story can be found in *Jesus and the storm*, Bible Societies, or *Storytime 1*, page 75, Scripture Union.
Aim to show the power of Jesus and his willingness to help us in every situation. Remind the children first of what a storm is like and how frightened people might feel.

Prayer Thank you, Jesus, for taking care of the men in the boat. Thank you for helping them when they were worried. Thank you for looking after me when I am afraid. Amen.

Song   'God takes good care of me' (first 2 verses). *Come and Sing*, Scripture Union.

OR   'Jesus is the best friend'. *Come and Sing*, Scripture Union. (another verse could be added –
Jesus is the best Friend
I know that he loves me
He helps me when I feel afraid
I'm glad that he loves me.)

9TH DAY   RECAP OF PREVIOUS ASSEMBLIES ON THE THEME OF WATER

Play some of the music again, eg 'Fingal's Cave'. Look at work produced by the children, eg chart made by a child to show how much water he uses in one day; a child's book of water experiments; a child's poem about the sea; a painting of a lifeboat etc.

Prayer   Children read their own prayers about the sea or rain.
Song   'I'm very glad of God'. *Someone's Singing, Lord*, A & C Black.

Earth

1ST DAY   ROCKS

Have a collection of stones and pieces of rock – if possible a variety including granite, sandstone, limestone. Ask the children what they are a set of and explain that the earth we live on is made of rocks, covered with soil in places and covered with sea in many places. Look at a picture of mountains. Look at the shapes of the rocks. Ask a child to feel a piece and say whether it is hard or soft. Show that some are rough and jagged and others are smooth. Explain that little stones are called pebbles and ask children where they can be found – most will know they are often found on a beach and will enjoy hearing how the sea rubs the stones together until they get smaller and smaller, finally forming sand.

Prayer   Thank you, God, for making our world. Thank you for the huge mountains of rock and for the tiny grains of sand. We like to jump off big stones and dig at the seaside. We enjoy the world you have made. Amen.

Song 'God who made the earth'. *Sing to God*, Scripture Union.

2ND DAY   SOIL

Have a tray of soil and ask the children what it is – let them describe it; lumpy, brown, sometimes hard, sometimes crumbly, sometimes wet, sometimes dry. Ask where we find soil – in our gardens, in the park, in the woods etc. Explain there are rocks underneath with soil on top. Stress how useful the soil is because things grow in it. Ask the children what sort of things – trees, flowers, vegetables, corn. Establish which part of the plant is in the soil, perhaps using a picture of a tree. The branches and leaves are not in the soil, but the roots are. Explain how the roots get the sort of food plants need from the soil and the roots help to support the trees and flowers so that they stand up straight in the ground. Discuss caring for things growing in the soil.

Prayer   Thank you, God, for the soil that is so useful. Thank you for the trees and the flowers that grow in the soil. Please help us to take good care of them. Amen.

Song   'And God said'. *Come and Sing*, Scripture Union
OR   'Over the earth'. *Someone's Singing, Lord*, A & C Black.
Useful book: *Trees*, Life Cycle Books, Althea, Longmans

3RD DAY   ROOT VEGETABLES

Remind the children of the previous day's Assembly – how thankful we are for the soil. Have some root vegetables in a bag and choose children to come out one at a time and pick a vegetable out. Name each vegetable. Establish that you have a set of 'vegetables' and possibly the children might know what they have in common – they are vegetables that grow in the soil underground. We eat the *roots* of these plants – potatoes, carrots, parsnips, onions, beetroot – not the stems or leaves or flowers. Suggest children try printing with some root vegetables.

Prayer   Thank you, God, for all these good vegetables you have given to make us healthy and strong. Amen.

Song 'Thank you for the world so sweet'. *Hymns and Songs*, Lady-bird Books.

Useful story – *The Enormous Turnip*, Ladybird Books.

4TH DAY   VEGETABLES ABOVE GROUND

Remind the children of the set of root vegetables seen the previous day. Explain you have another set of vegetables and show cauliflower, lettuce, beans, cucumber, tomato etc. The older children might be able to say these are parts of the plant above the ground. The younger children will be more interested in naming them. Stress how fortunate we are to have so many different kinds of food growing for us to eat.

Prayer   Thank you, God, for the people who grow vegetables for us to eat, for the shopkeepers who sell them and for our Mums and Dads who get the food ready for us. Amen.

Song   'For health and strength'. *Sing to God*, Scripture Union.

Useful book: *Vegetables*, The Nature Table Series, Evans.

5TH DAY   FRUIT

Show children a set of fruit, using as many different ones as are available – apple, orange, grapefruit, banana, lemon, pear, peach. If they are not obtainable, pictures of some could be used. See if the children know which ones grow in our country and which ones we import. Children could learn the names 'orchard' (place with many apple trees) and 'plantation' (place where large numbers of bananas grow). Cut open some of the fruit to look at the seeds inside. Explain that a fruit is the part of the flower that grows containing seeds and how new plants grow from the seeds. Suggest children try to find out in the classroom which fruits have many seeds and which have few or only one. Some children might like to make a graph of favourite fruits.

Prayer   I like to bite a crispy apple.
I like to suck a juicy orange.
I like to feel the skins and see the tiny seeds inside.
Thank you for all kinds of fruit and the people who work hard to grow them for us. Amen.

Song   'And God said'. *Come and Sing*, Scripture Union.

OR   'See, here are red apples'. *Come and Sing*, Scripture Union.

This Assembly could be linked with the story *The Very Hungry Caterpillar*. Eric Carle, Puffin Books. (For younger children this may be more suitable than thinking about the places where different fruits are grown.)

6TH DAY CEREAL CROPS

Show children three different cereal crops in turn, wheat, barley, oats. (Explain the collective word for these is corn, as children are often confused by this term.) Give time for the children to see the different shape of these plants and discuss each in turn. The wheat stalks are used as bedding for animals and the grain is made into flour. Explain that each class will be given some grains, so they can have the experience of rubbing the grains between two heavy stones to find the flour inside. What do we do with flour? Let children give the answers – to be made into bread, biscuits, cake etc. The barley is hairy and the grains are used to make beer and as food for animals. Look at barley seeds. Oats quiver in the breeze and are grown mainly to be made into porridge. Show oats and see if children can describe the difference in shape from the other cereal grains. Ask the children to be thinking who it is who takes care of the soil, so that the cereal crops can grow – in preparation for the following Assembly about the farmer.
It may be a good idea to use the story *The Little Red Hen*, William Stobbs, O.U.P. instead of, or in addition to, the suggestions above, with the very youngest children.

Prayer Thank you, God, for sending the sun and the rain to make the wheat grow. Thank you for the flour in the grains of wheat. Thank you for our crusty loaves of bread. Amen.

Song 'Thank you for the world so sweet'. *Hymns and Songs*, Ladybird Books.

OR 'For health and strength and daily food'. *Sing to God*, Scripture Union.

7TH DAY THE FARMER

Remind the children that they have been thinking about the soil and the things that grow in it. God sends the sun, wind and the rain to make plants grow, but he needs the farmers to help him to take care of the soil. Some toy agricultural machinery could be used as a visual aid.

The farmer uses the plough in his fields to turn the earth over. Then he uses a harrow to break the soil into smaller lumps and make it just right for the seeds. Then he plants the seeds with a machine called a drill – he puts in all sorts of seeds – wheat in one field, maybe barley in another and so on.

Soon little shoots begin to grow – the plants grow taller and taller. Then it is ready to cut and the farmer uses his combine harvester. How fortunate we are to have farmers in our country working hard all the year round to take care of the soil.

Prayer   Thank you, God, for the farmers who grow food for us to eat. Thank you for all their hard work. Please help us to work hard at the jobs you have given us to do. Amen.

Song   'Harvest Song' 44, *Come and Sing Some More*, Scripture Union

OR   'When the corn is planted',

OR   'The farmer comes to scatter the seed', both in *Someone's Singing, Lord*, A & C Black.

8TH DAY   THE SOWER

Bible story   Matthew chapter 13, Mark chapter 4

This is a story Jesus told about a farmer. This farmer hadn't got a tractor or machines to help him work because it was a long time ago. He wanted to sow some seeds in the ground and he had a big basket full of tiny seeds. He held it in one hand and used the other hand to throw the seeds on to the ground – like this. The little seeds needed good soft earth where they could grow safely. As the farmer walked along scattering the seeds, some fell on the path at the edge of the field and do you know what happened? The hungry birds swooped down and ate them before they could grow – what a shame! Some of the seeds fell in stony places where there wasn't much earth – the soil wasn't very deep. The seeds began to grow, but there was no room for their roots to make the plant stand up straight in the soil. When the hot sun shone it scorched up the plants and they died – what a shame! These seeds didn't grow properly. The farmer went on scattering his seeds all over the field, some fell where there were thorns and thistles and when the little seeds began to grow the thorns and thistles were so tall that the sun and the rain couldn't reach the little plants beginning to grow, so they withered and died. That was sad, wasn't it? But some of the seed fell on good soil where there were no stones and no thistles. There was a lot of room to grow. The rain fell and the sun shone and the little roots grew down and the little shoots grew up taller and taller and very strong.

At the top of the plant was an ear of corn (show one) with lots of little seeds of its own, growing on a stalk. The farmer was very pleased. The seeds on the path and the seeds among the stones and the seeds near the thistles were no use at all, but the seeds that grew in the good soft brown soil became useful plants.

Jesus wants us to be like the plants that grew up and became useful.

Prayer Dear Lord Jesus, please help me to grow up into a useful person. Show me ways to work for you. Amen.

Song 'Hands to work'. *Someone's Singing, Lord*, A & C Black.

9TH DAY MINERALS

Remind the children that everyone in the school has been thinking about the good earth that God has given us – the rocks, the soil and the things that grow in it, and today we think about other things we find in the earth – very often deep down underneath the ground. These things are usually so deep in the earth that men have to go down a long way to fetch them for us – these things are called minerals. Show some to the children one at a time, naming each and asking what each one is used for.

Iron ore – used for many purposes – steel is made from it and then used to make bridges and aeroplanes and railway lines; also knives, forks and spoons.

Coal – men go down pit shafts in lifts called cages and machinery is used to help them take out the coal – the men are called miners. (Show pictures of a miner with miner's lamp.) Explain that it is dark, dirty and can be dangerous work. Coal is used in electricity and gas industries.

Salt – not so difficult to mine.

Diamonds and gold – usually a teacher will lend a wedding or engagement ring for a short period! How strange that such a beautiful thing came from under the ground.

Prayer Heavenly Father, today we remember all the miners who work underground, sometimes in dangerous places. Please keep them safe and help them to work hard. Thank you for the useful and beautiful things they find for us. Amen.

Song 'Hands to work'. *Someone's Singing, Lord*, A & C Black.
'God of concrete, God of steel'. (first verse only), *Sing to God*, Scripture Union.

Other prayers from *The Lion Book of Children's Prayers*, page 64, 'Dear God. . . .' and 'Please bless. . . .'

The book *The story of steel* may be useful, First Facts, Sidgwick & Jackson, London.

Air

1ST DAY AIR ALL AROUND US

All around us there is air. Can you see it? Take a handful; can you feel it? Take a mouthful – can you taste it? Blow on your hand to make a little wind – now can you feel it? Establish with the children that air is all around us but we can't see it or smell it or taste it; we can only feel it when it is moving about. Also establish that if there is a wind, although you cannot see it, you *can* see what it does – eg it blows the trees and you can see the movement of the branches and leaves, you can see the clouds moving across the sky. The children could think of these and other examples. Explain this is like God. We cannot see him, but we can see what he is doing – we can see him helping someone to be kind and we can see him helping someone to say they are sorry and we can certainly see all the beautiful things he has made.

Prayer Dear Father God, I can't see the air, but I know it is all around me. I can't see you but I am glad you are with me everywhere. Amen.

Song 'I can't see the wind'. *Come and Sing*, Scripture Union.

2ND DAY THE USES OF AIR

Air is very useful – it is in fact essential, as we need air to breathe. Let the children put their hands on their chests and feel the air filling up their lungs. Explain that all living creatures need air. The older children would enjoy carrying out some experiments or being told about them, so they are able to do them later in the classroom with their own teachers.

Hold a jam jar to your ear and listen. Can you hear anything? What might it be? (Air moving about inside the jar.)

Stand a candle in a bowl of water. Light it, watch it burn – then cover the lighted candle with a jam jar and watch the candle go out. Why does it go out? What happens to the water and why? (The burning candle uses up some of the air and the water rises to take its place.) The younger children could think about how useful air is, because things can fly in it. Let them make suggestions – birds, butterflies etc. These things fly because they have wings. God designed them especially that way. People watched the birds flying and made aeroplanes – they copied God's design.

Prayer (Remind the children before they pray that just as the air is all around us, so is God's love.)
We know the air is all around us. Thank you, God, that your love is all around us too.
You are with us when we get up each morning. You are with us at school in our work and play. You are with us as we go back to our homes and when we are safely tucked up in bed. Amen.

Song 'God who made the earth' *Sing to God*, Scripture Union.

3RD DAY INSECTS THAT FLY

Play some of the music 'Flight of the bumble bee' by Rimsky-Korsakov. Ask the children if it reminds them of something that flies. Establish it is music about a bee and explain how useful bees are, concentrating especially on the fact that bees give honey. Show pictures of other insects which fly and with older infants explain that all insects have a skeleton-like suit of armour on the outside, three pairs of legs, two pairs of wings and that they lay eggs. The children would enjoy looking at various insects under a magnifying glass (left out somewhere for them to see). Show some pictures of butterflies and encourage the children to wonder at how delicate and beautiful they are. How amazing that God took such care over a creature that sometimes only lives one day. Show the children how to make butterfly pictures from blobs of paint on a folded piece of paper.

Prayer Thank you, Father God, for all the care you took in making tiny creatures. We thank you for their beautiful colours and their delicate wings. Amen.

Song 'All things bright and beautiful'. *Sing to God*, Scripture Union.
The book *Butterflies*, Althea, Longmans, may be useful.

4TH DAY BIRDS

Children could hold up paintings or collage pictures of birds they have seen around school or at home. Ask children what it is that all birds have or all birds do. They have feathers and beaks, they lay eggs in a nest, most can fly (not ostrich, emu or penguin). Show children a bird's nest, feathers and an egg. Suggest that the children listen to bird songs.

Part of a record or tape could be played eg 'Garden and Park Birds', Shell Nature Record. Explain how God cares for the birds. The Bible says that he knows when a little sparrow falls to the ground.

Ask the children how they can help to care for birds – feed them in the winter and give water, always leave eggs in a nest if they find one, leave a baby bird just where it is, as the parent will come back to find it.

Suggest that some children might observe birds to find out what they eat, how they move on the ground and whether or not there is anything special about the way they fly. These observations could be brought back to another Assembly.

Prayer Thank you, God, for birds, for their beautiful colours and cheerful songs. Help us to take care of them. Amen.

Song 'This is a lovely world'. *Someone's Singing, Lord*, A & C Black.

OR 'Little birds in winter time'. *Someone's Singing, Lord*, A & C Black.

The book *Birds*, Althea, Longmans, may be useful.

5TH DAY THE SKY

Children could show pictures or read their own writing about things that we see in the sky – birds, butterflies, kites, aeroplanes etc. Explain to the children that the sky is just a big space full of air. It has no colour and is all round the earth: like a cover which keeps the earth from getting too cold at night or too hot by day. Discuss the changing colour of the sky – blue on a lovely sunny day, black at night, pink sometimes at sunrise or sunset. Think about the clouds, fluffy and white sometimes, or dark grey before rain. Explain how the clouds are made up of little drops of water which fall as rain. Sometimes you can hear the air moving about and bumping and we call that thunder. Ask the children if they have ever seen a rainbow – what colours? – red, orange, yellow, green, blue, indigo, violet). It says in the Bible that a rainbow is to remind us about how much God loves us.

Prayer from *The Lion Book of Children's Prayers* beginning 'Praised be our Lord for the wind and the rain', page 61.

OR We praise you, Lord, for the blue sky on a sunny day, for the black sky dotted with twinkling stars at night, for the fluffy white clouds constantly changing shape and the colourful rainbow which reminds us of how much you love us. Amen.

Song 'God who made the earth'. *Sing to God*, Scripture Union.

OR 'Over the earth is a mat of green'. *Someone's Singing, Lord*, A & C Black.

Fire

1ST DAY USES OF FIRE

Some of the children will be looking forward to being Cub-Scouts or Brownie-Guides. If so, they will probably be able to tell the others about camp-fires – finding a safe place and collecting sticks etc. Others will have seen their parents making a bonfire in the garden to burn the garden rubbish. Explain that many years ago that was the only way people could keep warm and cook their food. What do we have now, usually, to keep our homes warm and for cooking? Establish that some people have coal fires, others have central heating. We cook on gas cookers or electric cookers. Remind the children that the caretaker keeps the school warm.

Prayer Thank you, God, for our warm homes and our warm school. Thank you for the clever people who make our cookers and radiators. Amen.

Song 'God takes good care of me'. *Come and Sing*, Scripture Union.

2ND DAY FIREWORKS

Play some of 'The Music for the Royal Fireworks' by Handel. Ask children for names of fireworks and words to describe them – both sight and sound, eg sparkly, glittering, whoosh, whizz, explode etc. Children could show firework pictures made with chalk on black paper.
Poems to read – 'November the Fifth' by Leonard Clark. *Young Puffin Book of Verse*, Penguin. 'Please to Remember', Walter de la Mare, *Rhyme Time*, Hamlyn.

Prayer Thank you, Father God, that flames and fireworks can be very beautiful to see and hear, flickering, darting and shooting out twinkling coloured stars, then sinking to the earth. Please help me to remember that fire can also be very dangerous. Please make me listen to my parents and teachers when they tell me about fire, so that nobody gets hurt. Amen.

Song 'I'm very glad of God'. *Someone's Singing, Lord*, A & C Black.

3RD DAY FIREMEN AND THEIR WORK

This Assembly would follow on naturally after a visit to the fire station or after firemen have been to school during a fire practice. The children could show pictures, read about it etc. There would be a chance to use new vocabulary such as hose, hydrant, turntable ladder, and to stress all the hard and sometimes dangerous work firemen do for the community.

Prayer from *The Lion Book of Children's Prayers*, page 65. 'Dear God, we pray for the workers of the world. . . .'

Song 'Hands to work and feet to run'. *Someone's Singing, Lord*, A & C Black.

Light

1ST DAY SUN

We have no lights on in school today – how can we see? Where is the light coming from? Establish that the sun is the main source of light. It is really like a great ball of fire. When there are no clouds to cover the sun, we have a sunny day. Some children could tell others what they like to do on a sunny day or show pictures – going for a picnic, swim in the sea, play in the garden etc. Suggest activities for the children to try out later such as making pictures from black paper and tissue paper which can be stuck on a window, so the light can shine through. One of these could be shown as an example. Remind the children that they can see their shadows on a sunny day; sometimes short, sometimes long. Suggest they find out at which time of day the shadows are shortest and at which time they are longest. Older infants would enjoy finding out where the sun rises and where it sets.

Poem 'Sunning', page 107 in *Young Puffin Book of Verse*, Penguin Books.

Prayer Thank you, Father God, for the sun that gives us warmth and light. Thank you for all the fun we can have on sunny days playing outside with our friends. Amen.

Song 'I love the sun'. *Come and Sing*, Scripture Union.

OR 'We praise you for the sun'. *Someone's Singing, Lord*, A & C Black.

2ND DAY MOON

There is something in the sky at night that helps us to see. What is it?
Show a picture of the moon. Think about the different shapes of the
moon – sometimes it is circular, sometimes crescent-shaped. Also
discuss the colour and its beauty.
Show pictures of men on the moon, called astronauts, and give children
the opportunity to say how they got there. Explain there is no air on the
moon so the men needed to take air and food with them.

Poems   'Intruder' by Clive Sansom, *Young Puffin Book of Verse*,
Penguin.
'Is the moon tired?' Rossetti, *Book of 1000 Poems*, Evans.
Prayer   Thank you, God, for the silver moon that gives us light at night
time. Amen.
Song   'I love the *sun*' (changing the word sun to *moon*). *Come and
Sing*, Scripture Union.
OR   'Father we thank you for the night'. *Someone's Singing, Lord*,
A & C Black.

3RD DAY STARS

'Praise him, sun and moon,
praise him all you shining stars.' Psalm 148.
Group of children play 'Twinkle, twinkle, little star' on triangles with
piano. Before they play, ask the rest of the children to guess what
Assembly is about today. Explain that the stars are a *very* long way
away and that is why they seem so small. They make patterns in the
sky called constellations. Remind the children that The Wise Men
followed a special star when they were looking for Jesus.
Read Poem. 'The Night Sky'. *Book of 1000 Poems*, Evans.

Prayer   Thank you, God, for the twinkling stars in the night sky. We
are asleep when the stars are shining. Sometimes our
bedrooms are dark and we feel a little bit afraid. Help us to
remember that you are caring for us all the time. Amen.
Song   'God who put the stars in space'. *Come and Sing*, Scripture
Union.
OR   'Can you count the stars?' *Someone's Singing, Lord*, A & C
Black.
OR   'Father we thank you for the night'. *Someone's Singing, Lord*,
A & C Black.

4TH DAY   ARTIFICIAL LIGHT

On a dark winter's day or at night time when we have drawn the curtains, how do we light our homes? You can turn on a switch in your house and have electric light. I expect Mummy or Daddy has to put new bulbs in your lights sometimes. Ask the children where else they have seen electric light – traffic signals, lighthouses, in cars, film projectors etc. Remind the children what happens in a power cut when we have no electricity – have they lit candles in their houses? Explain how fortunate we are to have electric light most of the time, as many parts of the world do not. Some people have to burn logs or oil or candles whenever they need light.
The children would enjoy learning how to make shadow puppets on a wall using a torch.

Prayer   We are glad, loving Father, that we have electric light in our homes. When it is dark outside, we can still play with our toys inside and look at our books. Please bless all the people who work hard so that we can have lights in our homes. Amen.

Song   'Loving Father of all children', *Come and Sing*, Scripture Union.

5TH DAY   THE LOST COIN

Bible story   Luke chapter 15, verses 8–10
I wonder if you have ever lost anything you especially liked – maybe a small toy or a piece of a game that was spoilt without all the pieces being there? You must have felt very sad and I expect you looked everywhere for it. I hope you found it.
There was once a lady who had something *very* precious – that means she couldn't have replaced it and got another one. I'll tell you about it. This lady had recently been married to a man she loved very much. The wedding was a lovely day. She had new clothes with silver and gold thread that sparkled. Her Mummy and Daddy had dressed up too because it was a special day and lots of friends came to see her being married. There were lots of lovely things to eat and drink and there was a party with music and dancing. But – the best part of all was that her new husband gave her a *very* special present. It was a band to wear round her head with ten little silver coins hung on it. It looked a bit like this (milk bottle tops cut smaller and threaded on a string). The coins glittered as she moved her head. Everyone thought it was lovely. When she took off the band, she always put it somewhere very safe, because it was so special. One day the lady was working in her house – she

cooked and cleaned, just like your Mummy does and then she got ready to go out. She wanted to wear her special headband so she went to the big chest where it was kept. But, when she got it out, there was something missing. There were only nine coins instead of ten. She counted again to make sure (let children join in, having first removed one). Oh dear, she had lost one of her precious coins. The lady felt very sad and started at once to hunt for it. Her house was quite dark because the windows were small and she didn't have electric light as you have – so it was very difficult to look for one little coin. She looked everywhere but couldn't find it. She even got her broom out again and swept the floor, but the coin was nowhere to be found. She felt like crying because the coin was so precious. Then she thought, 'I wonder if it has rolled into a dark corner and I can't see it. I know, I'll light my oil lamp.' (Show picture of one, if a suitable one is not available.) She did this and very carefully peeped into all the dark corners with her lamp and at last there in the darkest corner something was glinting – yes, it was her missing coin. She picked it up and rubbed off the dust and just held it in her hand. Then she felt so glad that she ran round to the lady next door and to all her friends and said, 'I've found my lost coin!' They were very pleased too and watched her fasten it back on her headband. The lady was so pleased to have it again.

Jesus told that story and he said that he is happy like that lady when we love him and want to please him. That makes Jesus very glad.

Prayer   Thank you, Lord Jesus, that you love us all very much. Please help us to make you happy today, because we love you and want to obey you. Amen.

Song   'Praise him, praise him'. *Come and Sing*, Scripture Union.
OR   'Wide, wide as the ocean'. *Sing to God*, Scripture Union.

6TH DAY PEOPLE WHO WORK AT NIGHT

When you are in bed at night, tucked up cosily, there are some people who are working. They sleep during part of the day, so they can help to take care of us at night. Ask the children to think of people who work at night – doctors, nurses, policemen, firemen, lighthouse keepers, night watchmen etc. Encourage the children to think why these people need to be awake. Discuss shift work if this is within the children's experience.

Prayer   Page 64, second prayer, in *The Lion Book of Children's Prayers*, beginning 'O God, help us to remember. . . .'
OR   Thank you, God, for all the men and women who work for us

during the night, so that we may be safe and have all the things we need. Please help them, especially when they are lonely or are feeling very tired. Amen.

Song   'Father, we thank you for the night'. *Someone's Singing, Lord*, A & C Black.

OR   'God who made the earth'. *Sing to God*, Scripture Union.

Natural materials

1ST DAY CLAY

Children show some things they have made using clay. Look at a lump of clay and explain how it comes from the ground. One child could show how to make a thumb pot, followed by discussion on use of a kiln. Show children some things made by adults – cup and saucer, vase, pottery figure etc. Emphasise how, although a china ornament may look much more beautiful than a plain kitchen mixing bowl, the bowl is however much more useful. Explain that *we* can be useful even though we may not look very special.

Prayer We thank you, God, for clay which can be used to make dishes and bowls and vases. Help us to be careful when we are touching delicate and beautiful things. Thank you for our hands that can make things. Please use our hands to make lovely, good and useful things. Amen.

Song 'Hands to work'. *Someone's Singing, Lord*, A & C Black.

2ND DAY SAND

Have two bowls, one containing dry sand and the other wet sand. Ask the children where sand is usually found – around the edge of the sea and in very dry places called deserts. Show how sand is formed by pebbles rubbing together. Each little bit is called a grain. A few children could let the dry sand trickle through their fingers. Explain how God knows the number of grains of sand on the sea-shore – how wonderful! Ask the children what they like to do with wet sand – make castles, dig tunnels etc. Recall the enjoyment experienced. Sand is fun to play in, but it is also useful. Builders use it for making cement. It is used for making glass too.

Prayer Thank you, God, for the fun we have playing in the sand. Thank you for castles we can build and the feeling of sand on our bare toes. Amen.

Song 'God made the shore'. *Come and Sing*, Scripture Union.

3RD DAY   THE TWO HOUSES

Bible story   Luke chapter 6, verses 46–49
Remind the children that they looked at sand the previous day and thought about the fun they have playing in it.
Explain to the children you have a story about two men and each one wanted to build a house. If you were looking for a good place to build a house you would need ground that was firm and solid, so the house would stand up properly. It wouldn't be a good place to build a house on the sand.
Read the story:– *The Two Builders*, Storytime 2, Scripture Union. Tell the children that Jesus told that story, but it would be best not to attempt to explain the meaning to such young children.

Prayer   Lord Jesus, thank you that your ideas are always best. Please help me to do the things you want every day. Amen.
Song   'The wise man built his house upon the rock' (with actions), *Scripture Union Choruses*, Scripture Union.
OR   in *Okki-tokki-unga*, A & C Black.

4TH DAY   COAL

Show children some coal (many will not have seen it before). Discuss how it comes from under the ground. Older infants will be interested to know how it was formed. (Forests of ferns in tropical swamps, covered in mud and water and under pressure, after millions of years, formed coal.) Show a picture of a miner, explaining why he wears a lamp on his head and how he goes down a pit shaft in a lift called a cage. The miners use machines to dig out the coal and it is hard work, and can sometimes be dangerous. Coal is used to help us keep warm (used in electricity and gas industries and in making of iron and steel).

Prayer   Thank you, God, for the coal miners who work hard under the ground to bring us our coal. Please help them in their work and keep them safe each day.
Song   'Hands to work'. *Someone's Singing, Lord*, A & C Black.
OR   'God of concrete'. *Sing to God*, Scripture Union.
Older infants may be interested and amused to see a set of things that come from coal – nylon tights, perfume, aspirin, antiseptic, paint, fertiliser, varnish, food flavourings!

5TH DAY   OIL

A few children could show box models of cars, vans, buses, aeroplanes. Ask the children what we need to make these things travel; what do we put into a car? Explain that petrol is made from oil. Oil comes from under the land sometimes, or from under the sea. The oil cannot go straight into cars and buses and aeroplanes, but has to be made right for them so that they can travel properly. Show pictures of a garage with petrol pump and an airport with an aeroplane being refuelled. A sound effect record could be used, 'City traffic' or 'Aeroplanes', EMI.

Prayer   Thank you, God, for oil. We like to ride in cars and buses and aeroplanes.
Please take care of all the men who work hard, so that we can travel about. Amen.

Song   'Things we enjoy', *Come and Sing*, Scripture Union.

Older infants might like to hear how the oil is extracted, put in storage tanks and travels along pipelines to the refinery. From here it is transported by ship, an oil tanker, usually very large with a red flag to show it is carrying dangerous cargo. The tankers discharge oil at storage installations and it is distributed by rail or road to petrol pumps, factories, airports etc.

6TH DAY   THE TEN BRIDESMAIDS

Bible story   Matthew chapter 25, verses 1–13

An introduction will be needed to establish that the children understand the words bride, bridegroom, bridesmaids. Probably there will be a child with recent experience of a wedding who could tell the others about it. The children will also need to know that people used to have oil lamps. It may be possible to show one, otherwise a picture of one will be needed. Aim to show that the five wise girls were ready and the five foolish girls had not bothered to get ready. A useful book is *We couldn't be bothered*, Church House Publishing, Rainbow Books.

Prayer   Lord Jesus, sometimes I am slow getting ready to go out and keep my family waiting. Sometimes I say, 'I can't be bothered,' when Mummy or my teacher reminds me to do something. Please help me to do quickly the things that are sensible and good and useful. Amen.

Song   'For the things that I've done wrong'. *Come and Sing*, Scripture Union, followed by second verse of 'Father we thank you for the night'. *Someone's Singing, Lord*, A & C Black.

7TH DAY   WOOD

Show children a set of wooden things, including objects used every day, such as a wooden spoon, but also something beautiful such as a carved wooden figure or animal. Ask the children what is the same about all the objects you have in front of you and establish that they are all made from wood. Some things might lend themselves to further discussion, eg children could describe the colour, shape, texture etc. Wood comes from trees (show picture). Lumberjacks fell the trees and take off the branches. The wood is then used to make many things we see each day. Ask the children to think of wooden furniture in their home and suggest they see how many things in their classrooms are wooden. Look at a wooden model made by a child and maybe some of the tools used to make it. Remind the children Jesus was a carpenter.

Prayer   Thank you, God, for men and women who have carefully made things out of wood and taken a long time to make the very best they could. Help us to work hard at the things we make. Amen.

OR   Thank you, God, for trees. Sometimes I climb into the branches and peer at the sky through the leaves. Thank you for the shade trees give on a hot day. Thank you for the wood, used for so many good and useful things. Amen.

Song   'Over the earth is a mat of green'. *Someone's Singing, Lord*, A & C Black.

A group of children could show bark rubbings.

8TH DAY   BOOKS FROM WOOD

Have some books on display and a variety of paper. Explain that paper is made from wood.
Read the story *Thank you for a book to read*, Lion Publishing.

Prayer   Dear God, thank you for books. Thank you for the people who write them and the people who read them to us. Thank you for picture books and story books, for ones that make us laugh and others which tell us interesting things. Thank you most of all for stories about Jesus. Amen.

Song　'Tell me the stories of Jesus'. *Sing to God*, Scripture Union (first verse only).

9TH DAY   RUBBER

Show children a set of rubber objects – tyre, ball, glove, wellington boots, hot water bottle, elastic band etc. Encourage children to say they are all made from rubber. Explain how rubber comes from a giant rubber tree which has a liquid in it called latex. This is collected from the trees in a process called tapping. A picture would be useful here. Think about how useful rubber things are as they are waterproof (this word may need explaining to the children).

Prayer　I like to splash in puddles in my wellington boots. I like to bounce my rubber ball. I like to snuggle up in bed with a hot water bottle. Thank you, God, for rubber. Amen.

Song　'This is the day'. *Come and Sing Some More*, Scripture Union.

10TH DAY   COTTON

Show children some articles made from cotton – dress, handkerchief, shirt. Choose some children wearing cotton clothes to stand at the front. Tell children that cotton comes from a plant. The cotton plant does not grow in our country. Show a picture of what it looks like and explain how the cotton is the part protecting the seeds, how it is picked and packed in bales and then carried in ships to other countries. It needs to be made into threads – (show a thread of cotton) – and then woven, dyed and printed. This will be more easily understood if the children have had the experience of weaving with paper strips or old tights etc.
Suggest the children look under a magnifying glass at some cotton material to see the threads.
Find out if the children know when we usually wear cotton clothes and why.

Prayer　Thank you, God, for the people in countries far away who grow cotton plants. Thank you for my cotton clothes which help to keep me cool on a hot day. Amen.

Song　'He's got the whole wide world in his hands'. *Sing to God*, Scripture Union.

11TH DAY 'THANK YOU FOR A PAIR OF JEANS',
Lion Publishing

This is a link with the previous day's Assembly and could be used either as a follow-up or on its own, leaving out 10th day.

12TH DAY   WOOL

Show children a set of woollen things – sheepskin coat, jumper, gloves, blanket etc. Have some knitting on needles – does your Mum or Granny knit you cardigans and mittens? They use wool and all these things are made of wool. Where does wool come from? Show a picture of a sheep and if possible some natural wool, so the children can feel how soft it is and how greasy. Show a picture of sheep-shearing or explain how this is done, making sure the children know that it does not hurt the sheep (like us having a hair-cut!). The wool from the sheep needs to be cleaned, so that all the grease is taken out and then it needs to be made into threads, so we can have warm jerseys to wear on a cold day. One or two children wearing woollen garments could be visual aids.

Prayer   Thank you, God, for our warm woollen clothes to wear in winter-time. Thank you for all the people who look after sheep and make their wool into things for us to wear. Amen.

Song   'All things bright and beautiful'. *Sing to God*, Scripture Union.

13TH DAY   THE LOST SHEEP

Bible story   Luke chapter 15, verses 1–7
Aim to show that the Shepherd knew all his sheep and loved each one. Have a picture of sheep and lambs on display, so you can be sure before the story that the children know the meaning of the words – sheep, lamb, shepherd, crook.
There was once a good, kind, shepherd who had one hundred sheep. He knew every one of them and loved them all. He took them to places where there was juicy grass to eat. If the sheep or lambs got scratched he took the prickles out of their wool. On hot days he found streams where they could have cool water to drink. Every night he counted them to make sure they were all safe – 1, 2, 3 right up to 97, 98, 99, 100. He loved his sheep and was glad they were safe.
One day the good, kind shepherd took out all his sheep and lambs as

usual. There was one lamb who was very interested in everything around him and instead of keeping with the other sheep he thought he would like to go exploring on his own. He found some juicy grass and thought, 'I like this.' So he went further to find some more. All the other sheep and lambs, with the kind shepherd, went a different way. The little lamb liked it at first, but soon the ground became bumpy and hard to walk on. There were big stones and big holes and the little lamb began to wish he had stayed with the other sheep and the good, kind shepherd. Then something *very* sad happened; the little lamb slipped on a big stone and fell into a hole. He couldn't climb out and it was getting dark. He was tired, alone and very frightened.

I wonder what the good, kind shepherd was doing? He was making sure all his sheep were safe for the night. He began to count them, 1, 2, 3 . . . 96, 97, 98, 99 – oh dear, only 99. There was one missing. The kind shepherd knew just which one it was. 'My dear little lamb is missing, so I must go and find him at once.' The shepherd took a lamp, so that he could see in the dark and a special stick called a crook. He looked first near the stream but the lamb was not there. Then he looked in the place where the juicy grass grew, but he wasn't there. He called but there was no answer. He looked in the thorn bushes, but the lamb was not there. Then the kind shepherd came to a place where there were big stones and big holes. He heard a little 'baa'. 'There he is,' said the shepherd and bent over the hole. Very carefully he lifted the lamb out with his crook. He stroked him gently and then put him on his shoulder to carry him home. How glad the lamb was to see the kind shepherd. How glad the good shepherd was to find the little lamb, because he loved all his sheep even when they were silly and wandered away. He was *such* a good, kind shepherd, wasn't he? I'll tell you something very special. Jesus loves us, just like the shepherd loved his little lamb. Jesus loves you and me and everyone.

Prayer Thank you, Jesus, for loving me always, even when I am silly and naughty. Thank you for loving all my family, and friends too. Amen.

Song 'Jesus is the best friend'. *Come and Sing*, Scripture Union.
OR 'Jesus loves me'. *Hymns and Songs*, Ladybird Books.

14TH DAY SILK

Have pictures of moths and caterpillars on display. Show children a silk scarf. Explain to the children that there is a special sort of caterpillar that makes silk threads. Tell them to think how thin the strands are in a spider's web – the strands of silk are like that. The special caterpillar is called a silkworm. (Show picture) It eats mulberry leaves and makes a little cocoon of silk around itself – this is wound onto bobbins and woven. How amazing that a little caterpillar should be able to help us make a beautiful silk scarf. This Assembly is only appropriate if the children in the school have had firsthand experience of keeping caterpillars, watching them pupate and seeing moths or butterflies emerge.

Prayer Thank you, God, for making tiny creatures like caterpillars. Please help me to be kind to the small insects and animals that you have made. Amen.

Song 'If I were a butterfly'. *Come and Sing Some More*, Scripture Union.

15TH DAY LEATHER

Display some pictures of cows, crocodiles, snakes, goats – and let the children identify them.
Show children a set of leather goods – shoes, handbag, purse, jacket, gloves. These are all made of leather. Leather is made from the skins of animals and it is usually very strong and waterproof, so the rain cannot soak through. The outside skin of a cow is called hide. It is put in a special liquid to make it soft, so that people can make us shoes to wear. Let a child with new shoes show them.

Prayer Thank you, God, for our strong leather shoes that keep out the cold and the rain. Amen.

Explain to the children that a lot of cows and bulls together are called *cattle*. God said, 'I own the cattle on a thousand hills.' He meant that everything in the world belongs to him and we are just helping to take care of his animals.

Song 'He's got the whole wide world in his hands'. *Sing to God*, Scripture Union.

Work

1ST DAY   OUR HOMES

Some children could show pictures of the places where they live; houses, flats, bungalows. We call the place where we live our 'home'. There are many jobs that need to be done in a home. We need to keep it clean. We need to get meals ready. We also want to make sure that all the people in our home are feeling happy. Some children could have prepared pictures and paintings about how they help at home. If not, they could suggest some ideas, eg – lay the table, dry the spoons and put them away, clear toys away at bedtime, help to clean the car etc. Make sure the ideas are really within the scope of an infant-aged child.

Prayer   Thank you, God, for our homes. Thank you for Mummy and Daddy, for brothers and sisters. Please help me to think of ways of helping my family at home. Amen.

Song   'Hands to work'. *Someone's Singing, Lord*, A & C Black.
OR   'Be kind'. *Come and Sing*, Scripture Union.

Some older infants might like to tell the younger ones about homes in other countries; houses made from different materials. The people in them still need to help each other.

2ND DAY   JESUS AT HOME

Remind the children of the pictures they saw the previous day, showing the sort of homes they live in.

Jesus, when he was a boy, lived with his family in a place called Nazareth. He lived with Mary and Joseph and his brothers and sisters. Show a picture of the sort of house Jesus would have lived in; a white stone building with a flat roof and stairs outside leading onto the roof (just a simple picture could be drawn with felt pen on white paper). We have thought of ways you can help at home. Jesus helped in his home too. (The picture of the interior of an Eastern House by SPCK is useful.) There is no oven, so I expect Jesus helped to collect sticks to make a fire, so that Mary could cook the meals. Jesus and his family did not have beds like ours; they slept on mats and I am sure Jesus helped to roll up the mats every morning and put them away. I am sure Mary asked him sometimes to carry baskets of fruit on to the flat roof to dry in the sun. I expect there were hens and maybe a donkey to care for and Jesus would like to feed them every day.

The Bible says that Jesus was obedient; that means he did what his parents asked him to do.

Prayer Thank you, Lord Jesus, that you lived in a home with a family. Thank you that you know all about our homes. Please make us quick to do what our parents ask us to do. Amen.

Song 'Jesus was born in Bethlehem' (3rd verse only). *Come and Sing*, Scripture Union.

OR 'Quickly obey'. *Come and Sing*, Scripture Union.

3RD DAY PARENTS WORKING OUTSIDE THE HOME

There are many jobs that your Mummy and Daddy do for you at home, to keep your house warm and clean and to make sure you are comfortable. We have thought about how you can help.

Some of you have parents who go out to work; maybe Mummy or Daddy or both go out to do a job. Do any of you know what jobs they do? I wonder why they go out to work? Explain to the children that they earn money, so the family can have food and clothes and toys etc. When Mummy or Daddy get home from work, I expect they are tired, so maybe you could try to help by doing what they ask quickly. You could put your toys away without a fuss and put on your nightie or pyjamas when they ask you. Maybe there will be time then for a game or a story together.

Prayers Thank you, God, for all the people who work hard every day so that we can have all the things we need; food to eat, clothes to wear and warm comfortable homes.

Dear God, please help those who have no work. They must be bored and feel unhappy. Show them what they can do while they are waiting for a job and give them work to do soon. Amen.

OR The prayer on page 64 in *The Lion Book of Children's Prayers* beginning 'Dear God, please look after everyone at work today'.

Song 'For health and strength'. *Sing to God*, Scripture Union.

OR 'Father we thank you for the night'. *Someone's Singing, Lord*, A & C Black.

4TH DAY   JESUS HELPING IN THE CARPENTER'S SHOP

We have talked about the work your mothers and fathers do. Jesus liked to watch Mary and Joseph doing their work and helped them whenever he could. Joseph had a special job; do you remember what it was? He was a carpenter; he made things out of wood. Show some tools and explain that the ones Joseph had would not have been quite the same; hammer, saw, drill, chisel, plane, file and nails. Let a child show a model made from wood and explain that it was hard work. Joseph probably made big boxes called chests, wooden doors, ploughs for the farmers and wooden bowls. (Show a picture of the workshop – postcards of famous paintings and stained glass windows are useful.) I expect Jesus helped to sweep up the sawdust and sometimes he would hold the wood while Joseph used the saw. Joseph did his best work to make sure that things lasted a long time. It was hard work, so he needed to be strong. When Jesus grew up he became a carpenter too. He needed to be strong, but never rough.

Prayer   Thank you, Jesus, that you know all about hard work. Please help us to work hard at the jobs we are given to do. Help us to use our hands in gentle and kind ways. Amen.

Song   'For all the strength we have'. *Someone's Singing, Lord*, A & C Black.

OR   'Jesus' hands were kind hands'. *Someone's Singing, Lord*, A & C Black.

5TH DAY   PEOPLE WHO WORK IN OUR SCHOOL

We have thought about the work Mummy and Daddy do and how you help. Today we are going to think all about the people who work in our school. Can you think who they are? Let the children give suggestions and recap at the end, mentioning those the children may have forgotten, caretaker, cleaners, secretary, general assistants, cooks, dinner supervisors, teachers, children.
We are going to say thank you for all these people. Please join in 'We thank you' after each line. (Where possible it would be best to name the people and add any appropriate phrase.)

Prayer   For all the teachers who help us to learn interesting things (We thank you.)
For the caretaker and cleaners who sweep the floors and keep the school warm –
For the cooks who make our dinners –

For the dinner ladies who take care of us in the playground –
For our school secretary who types the letters and answers
the telephone –
For the general assistants who help us in so many ways –
For the school nurse and doctor who come to visit us –
Help all these people to work hard and do their best to make
our school a happy place.

Song 'Hands to work'. *Someone's Singing, Lord*, A & C Black.
'God made the people that I meet
The many people great and small
At home, at school and down the street
And he made me to love them all.' (From No. 9 *Someone's Singing Lord*, A & C Black.)

6TH DAY   JESUS AT SCHOOL AND OUR WORK AT SCHOOL

I know that all the *children* in this school work very hard. Give time for some children to show their work; a model, painting or story etc. Some children could tell about the things they like doing best at school.
When Jesus was a little boy he went to school. Only the boys went to school, not the girls, who stayed at home to help their mothers. Jesus learned to read, like you do, but his book opened in a different way. Make a scroll beforehand and show how it was unrolled. Jesus learned to write letters and numbers like you do, but he had no paper. He wrote with his fingers in the sand. Let a child sit on the floor with a tray of sand and demonstrate. Jesus worked hard and tried to do his best.
In our school some people are good at writing, some are good at skipping, some are good at listening to their teacher, some are good at making friends and being kind. Jesus wants us to do our best work and he will help us.

Prayer Lord Jesus, help us in our school work to do our best and to try to please you. Help us not to mind when we can't get something right; may we do it again cheerfully and carefully. Thank you for our minds that can think and plan and for all the interesting things we can make or do. Give us ideas that are good and useful and that will make other people happy. Amen.

Song 'God whose name is love'. *Hymns and Songs*, Ladybird Books.

53

7TH DAY   PEOPLE WE SEE WORKING EVERY DAY

While you are at school, learning to read and write and sew, while you are measuring and weighing, painting and building – there are many grown up people working to help us. I expect some people have already been to your house today – has someone brought anything to your house this morning? Discuss the work of the milkman and postman. Suggest that some of the older children could make a graph about the number of milk bottles left or they could bring envelopes delivered to their houses and look at stamps, date posted etc. Ask the children if they can think of someone who comes to take something away from their house – the refuse collector or dustman. Explain the importance of that work.

Poems to read, all by Clive Sansom in *Come Follow Me*, Evans. 'The Milkman', 'The Postman', 'The Dustman'.

The children will be able to think of many more people they see at work each day, but this of course will depend upon where the children live – shopkeeper, farmer, policeman, builder, road worker etc. It would be appropriate to invite some of these people into school to talk about their work, show uniforms etc. Aim to show that *all* jobs are important and we all need one another. This could develop into a series of Assemblies; each class in turn thinking about one person who works in the community – fireman, dentist etc. These Assemblies could include appropriate songs, drama or poetry.

Prayer   Thank you, God, for the postman who brings us letters and birthday cards. Thank you for the milkman who brings our milk and for the dustman who takes away the rubbish. We see many people working each day. Help us to remember that we all need each other. Amen.

OR   prayer from *The Lion Book of Children's Prayers*, page 65. 'Dear God, we pray for the workers of the world'.

Song   'Hands to work'. *Someone's Singing, Lord*, A & C Black.

8TH DAY   PEOPLE JESUS SAW AT WORK

You like to watch people working, so you can learn more about what they do. Jesus liked to watch people working too, when he was a boy. Have four children appropriately dressed to represent a carpenter, a potter, a fisherman and a shepherd. Discuss each in turn. Remind the children that Jesus would know a lot about the carpenter's work, because he watched Joseph and helped him. The child representing the carpenter could hold up some tools – wooden mallet, saw, chisel. The carpenter made chests for storage, ploughs for the farmer, wooden bowls and spoons.

In the village where Jesus lived he would sometimes like to watch a potter. The child representing the potter should be sitting on the floor with a lump of clay on a stone. Explain to the children that the potter would have a special stone which he turned with his feet on which he made pottery. He made jars and lamps, bowls and plates. Sometimes the shape was not right, so he needed to begin all over again. He decorated some of the things he made using shells, pebbles or bones. Suggest that the children might like to try making patterns on clay (eg pressing a shell into clay and lifting it off again).

Sometimes Jesus went out of the village a little way to see a shepherd working. The child representing the shepherd could hold a crook and a sling if available. Jesus would see the shepherd walking in front of the sheep, leading the way to find juicy grass for the sheep to eat and water for them to drink. He used his crook sometimes if a sheep slipped in a hole, to help him lift it out. He used his sling with a stone in it to frighten away the wild animals that might try to hurt the sheep. He cared for the sheep and made sure they were all safe.

Sometimes Jesus went down to the lake and watched the fishermen. The child representing the fisherman could be sitting pretending to mend his nets. (A piece of garden netting would serve the purpose.) The fishermen needed to be very strong. They went out at night in their boats to catch fish in large nets. When they came back they sorted their fish into baskets (paper fish could be used) and mended their nets ready for the next night. When he grew up some of Jesus' very best friends were fishermen.

If there is too much material here for one Assembly, one occupation could be considered each day for a week. Others that might be included are the farmer, builder, and a woman fetching water from the well.

Many of these occupations could be linked with a Bible story where appropriate.

Shepherd – The Lost Sheep. See section on 'Natural Materials'.

Fisherman – Storm on the lake. See section on 'Fear'.

Farmer – The Sower, or Ruth and Boaz. See section on 'Being the sort of person Jesus wants us to be'.

Builder – The houses built on rock and sand. See section on 'Natural Materials'.

Fetching water – The woman at the well. John chapter 4, verses 4–42 (selected parts).

Useful reference book: *The Book of Bible Knowledge*, Scripture Union.

Prayer Jesus, I can't do the difficult jobs grown up people do, but I can do little things to help other people. Please show me something kind and useful that I can do today. Amen.

9TH DAY   JESUS WORKING WITH HIS FRIENDS

Bible story   Luke chapter 5, verses 1–11

There were once two brothers named Peter and Andrew and two more brothers called James and John. They were all good friends and they had all met a very special person. They had met Jesus and Jesus loved them very much.

Peter and Andrew, James and John were fishermen. Every night they went out on the lake in their boats. They put their big fishing nets into the water and waited quietly for the fish to swim into the nets. Then slowly they pulled up the nets to see what they had caught. Sometimes there were many fishes and sometimes just a few. They stayed out on the lake in their boats until it was morning. Then they took their boats back to the shore to unload the fish and sell them. They always looked carefully at their nets to make sure they were clean and sometimes they had to mend holes in the nets too. One night the fishermen worked very hard putting out their nets and pulling them in lots of times, but they did not catch any fish at all. In the morning they went back to the shore and began to clean their nets. I expect they felt disappointed that they had no fish. As they were sitting near their boats they saw Jesus coming along the shore. There were lots of people with him because they all wanted to hear the stories he told. The people were all pushing, trying to get near the front. When Jesus saw his friends, the fishermen, he said, 'Do you think I could use your boat, Peter? If you rowed a little way from the shore I could sit in your boat and everyone would be able to hear my story.' Peter was glad Jesus wanted to use his boat and it was a very good idea because everyone could see Jesus and everyone could hear him. He told them about how much God loved them. At the end of the story I think Jesus must have noticed there were no fish in the boats, so he told Peter and Andrew, James and John to take their boats out into the deep water. Then Jesus said, 'Peter, let down your nets into the water.'

I expect Peter thought that was a strange thing to say, because daytime wasn't a good time for catching fish. 'But we fished all night,' said Peter, 'and we didn't catch anything.' Then Peter remembered that Jesus was a very special person and he thought it was best to do what Jesus said. So Peter and Andrew let down their nets, waited quietly and then began carefully to pull them up again. What a surprise they had, because the nets were full of fish. In fact there were so many fish that the nets began to break. Peter and Andrew called James and John. They quickly came in their boat and the four fishermen filled their boats with fish and took them back to the shore. They were amazed that Jesus knew just the right place to catch the fish.

Then Jesus said to them, 'Fishing is an important job, but I have another important job for you to do. Will you come and help me to tell all the people how much God loves them? Will you be my special helpers?' Peter, Andrew, James and John told Jesus that they did want to be his helpers. So they unloaded their fish, looked carefully at their nets and put them away. Then they left their boats and went with Jesus to be his special helpers and friends.

Prayer   Dear Lord Jesus, thank you for helping the fishermen. You know all about our work and want to help us. We are glad you will help us with difficult things. We are glad too that you wanted the fishermen to be your special helpers. Please make me a helper too. Amen.

Song   'Peter's brown boat'. *Come and Sing*, Scripture Union.

OR   'Now Jesus one day'. *Someone's Singing, Lord*, A & C Black.

Meals

1ST DAY THE FUN OF COOKING

A group of children could take something they have cooked into Assembly, eg tarts or buns. Let them tell the others about the ingredients used and maybe read a group book about it. This book would have been made by the group of children who had been cooking and would contain their pictures and writing. Introduce the words 'recipe' and 'recipe book'. Show some of the utensils, naming them and asking the children what they are used for – rolling pin, pastry cutter etc. Count the cakes.

Prayer Thank you, God, for the fun I have cooking at school and at home. I like to stir the mixture, roll the pastry and cut out shapes. I like to lick the spoon and smell the biscuits cooking in the oven. Amen.

Song 'Thank you for the world so sweet'. *Hymns and Songs*, Ladybird Books.

2ND DAY FAVOURITE FOODS

Beforehand one class could prepare some work on their favourite foods. The children could draw their favourite meal on a circular piece of paper like a plate. Suggest that each class makes a graph about their favourite food, using pictures from magazines or their own drawings. Which food is the most popular?

Sing a Prayer
'For health and strength and daily food we praise thy name O Lord'. *Sing to God*, Scripture Union.

Song 'See, here are red apples'. *Come and Sing*, Scripture Union.
Substitute other foods instead of those given where appropriate.

3RD DAY SPECIAL MEALS

A group of children could read their accounts of exciting meals they have enjoyed, eg – at a picnic or party, a meal in a café or hotel, eating round a camp fire or at a wedding. Other children could show pictures of these special occasions.

Sing a camp fire song, eg 'Camp fire's burning' and a birthday song 'Happy birthday to you' or any other birthday songs known by the children at your particular school.

Prayer Thank you, Lord Jesus, for parties and special meals. Thank you for the lovely food; for fish and chips and sausages on sticks, for jelly and ice cream and fizzy drinks. Thank you for the games we play and the clothes we wear on special days too. Amen.

Song 'This is a lovely world'. *Someone's Singing, Lord*, A & C Black.
OR 'For all the strength we have'. *Someone's Singing, Lord*, A & C Black.

4TH DAY THE WEDDING AT CANA

Bible story John chapter 2, verses 1–11
Aim to show that Jesus enjoyed meals and parties and emphasise the love of Jesus for a family on their special day and his power in putting right a difficult situation.
This story can be found in *Jesus at the Wedding*, The Bible Societies Talkabouts series.

Prayer Jesus, I am glad the people did what you told them at the wedding, so everyone could have a happy time. Please help me to do what you want every day. Amen.
Song 'Trust and obey'. *Sing to God*, Scripture Union.

5TH DAY JESUS AT A PICNIC

Bible story The boy with the loaves and fishes. John chapter 6, verses 1–13
Aim to show the boy's willingness to share what he had and the power of Jesus to use the food to feed so many people.
The story can be found in *Storytime 2*, page 68, Scripture Union.

Prayer Lord Jesus, please help me to share my toys and sweets with other children and not to keep things just for myself. Amen.

Song   'All that I have.' (First verse and chorus only) *Sing to God*, Scripture Union.

6TH DAY   JESUS AT A CAMP FIRE

Bible story   The breakfast on the beach. John chapter 21, verses 1–14

Aim to show the frustration of the fishermen when they caught no fish, their thrill at discovering that the man on the beach was Jesus, their joy being with him again and the fact that Jesus knew exactly what they needed.

I wonder if you have ever had a meal cooked out of doors, perhaps at a barbecue or a camp fire? If your big brothers or sisters are Scouts or Guides they probably make a fire on the ground using sticks, so that they can cook food on it. This story is about a very special breakfast round a fire. Do you remember Jesus had some special friends who were fishermen? When Jesus died and came alive again on Easter Day he did not stay with his friends all the time. Sometimes they were sad, because he was not there. One evening Peter said, 'Let's go fishing again.' So they got their boat and their nets ready and set out on the lake in the evening, which is a good time to catch fish. They threw out their net many times, all through the night, but they did not catch one single fish. It was very disappointing. Then the sky began to brighten because the morning had come. It was dawn. The fishermen were tired and cold and hungry. It was a little misty by the lakeside and as the boat drew nearer to the shore the fishermen saw someone on the beach. The person on the beach shouted, 'Have you caught anything?' 'Nothing,' the fishermen said. The stranger called again. 'Throw your net over on the right side of the boat and you will catch some fish.'

I expect the fishermen thought that was a strange thing to say. They had been fishermen for years and knew all about catching fish, but they did what he said. When they started to pull in the net it felt very heavy and they could see it was full of shiny, wriggling fish, so many that they could not pull in the net. John looked again at the stranger on the beach and then he recognised who it was. 'It's Jesus!' he said. When Peter heard that he slipped on his fisherman's tunic and jumped into the sea and swam towards the shore. The others dragged the net behind the boat and rowed it to the lakeside. When they reached the land there was a little fire burning on the beach with some fish cooking on it. Jesus told them to bring some of the fish they had caught, as he knew they would be very hungry, so Peter helped the others to pull the net ashore and when they counted the fish there were 153. Jesus said, 'Come and have some breakfast,' so they sat round the fire, drying their wet clothes and warming their cold hands. Jesus gave them sizzling fish and hot bread to eat and I think it must have been the best breakfast they had ever tasted. How pleased they were to be with Jesus again. Isn't it wonderful that Jesus knew all about their work and all about what they needed? He knows about our work too and about the things we need.

Prayer Suitable prayers can be found after story number 11 in *The Lion Book of Bible Stories and Prayers*, Lion Publishing.
OR Thank you for making that breakfast on the beach such a happy time for your friends, Lord Jesus. Thank you for knowing all about the things we need too. Amen.
Song 'Jesus is the best friend'. *Come and Sing*, Scripture Union.
OR 'God who made the earth'. *Sing to God*, Scripture Union.

7TH DAY MATTHEW'S PARTY

Bible story Luke chapter 5, verses 27–32
This story can be found in *Storytime 1*, page 58, Scripture Union.
Aim to show that Jesus loves people even when they do wrong things. He wants to be their friend and help them to do good things.

Prayer Dear Lord Jesus, sometimes I want to do wrong things. I am sorry. Thank you that you still want to be my friend. Please help me to do the right things. Amen.
Song 'Jesus is the best friend'. *Come and Sing*, Scripture Union.
OR 'I am very sorry, God'. *Come and Sing*, Scripture Union.

8TH DAY HOW ALL OUR FOOD COMES FROM THE EARTH

Aim to show the children that all our food comes directly or indirectly from the earth (soil) or the sea. Have some soil in a container, as you will constantly need to draw the children's attention to it. Choose about six children and let them in turn tell everyone their favourite food then trace it back to its source, eg ice cream made from milk, milk comes from a cow, cows eat grass, the grass feeds on the *soil*. Chips made from potatoes, potatoes get their food from the *soil*. Sausages are from a cow or a pig, cow eats grass, pig eats root crops, grass and roots get food from the *soil*.

Cornflakes made from corn, corn grows in *soil* etc.

Next time you eat your favourite food – remember it comes from the soil!

Prayer Thank you, God, for the soil. Thank you for all the food that grows in it. Make me always grateful for my daily food. Amen.

Song 'Thank you for the world so sweet'. *Hymns and Songs*, Ladybird Books.

OR 'I love the sun' (the verses about sun, rain and wind, as these help the plants to grow). *Sing to God*, Scripture Union.

9TH DAY HOW OUR FOOD REACHES US

Show the children a loaf of bread. Did you know that a lot of people helped to make this loaf and worked hard before I could buy it today at the shop? I have a story that tells us all about it.

Read – *Thank you for a loaf of bread*, Lion Publishing.

Prayer Thank you, loving Father God, for all the people who help to make my bread. Thank you for sending the sun and the rain. Thank you for the farmer and the miller and the baker. Thank you for the shopkeeper and for Mum and Dad bringing bread home for my tea. Amen.

Song 'For health and strength'. *Sing to God*, Scripture Union.

OR 'And God said'. *Come and Sing*, Scripture Union.

OR 'The farmer comes to scatter the seed'. *Someone's Singing, Lord*, A & C Black.

10TH DAY PEOPLE WHO ARE HUNGRY

I expect you have breakfast before you come to school and lunch at school or at home and tea after school? You might be very lucky and have a drink and biscuit at bedtime too! I wonder if Mum or Dad ever say, 'There isn't any breakfast today and no lunch and no tea'? You would be *very* hungry wouldn't you? In our country we are very lucky because the sun shines and the rain falls and the seeds grow, so we can have enough food to eat.

In some countries far away there are people who are hungry. Sometimes it doesn't rain enough and the seeds die. The cows haven't enough grass to eat. Sometimes the people don't know how to look after their soil. God wants everyone to be happy and have enough to eat. There are some kind people in our country who try to help the hungry people. They send seeds and tractors and people who will teach the hungry families about how to look after their soil. They help to make places where the water can be collected, after it has rained a lot, and stored until they need it.

Prayer Lord Jesus, we have such a lot to eat. Please help mothers and fathers, boys and girls and tiny babies who are hungry. Thank you for kind people who try to help them. Please teach us not to be greedy or wasteful. Show us if there is anything we can do to help. Amen.

Song 'Kum ba yah'. *Someone's Singing, Lord*, A & C Black, or *Sing to God*, Scripture Union (different words).

This Assembly might be followed up by suggesting something the children could do to help, eg join in one of the TV Blue Peter projects if appropriate; keep some pocket money to give to one of the relief agencies etc.

Colours

1ST DAY   RED

Have a set of red objects to show the children. Let them say what is the *same* about these things. See if the children can think of something that is always red – eg ripe tomato, telephone box, ruby, radish etc. Talk about how red often means danger; red traffic lights mean stop, red flag on a ship means it is carrying dangerous cargo etc. Read the poem 'What is red?' by Mary O'Neil in *Rhyme Time*, Hamlyn.

Prayer   Thank you, God, for bright colours that make our homes and school look cheerful. Thank you for our coloured crayons, our toys and our clothes, for gay balloons and the flickering lights of the fairground.

Song   'Praise him'. *Come and Sing*, Scripture Union.

2ND DAY   YELLOW

One class could be responsible for collecting and bringing a set of yellow things into Assembly. Divide the things into two sub-sets – those things which are always yellow and those that are not, eg 1st set: dandelion, buttercup, banana, lemon, grapefruit, yolk of an egg, picture of a duckling etc. 2nd set: cup, bead, book, pencil etc. Ask the children into which set each thing should be placed. Explain to the children that many varieties of flowers are yellow because the colour attracts bees.

Prayer   Thank you, God, for our eyes. We can sée the wonderful world you have made. We can look at picture books and watch television. Please specially bless those who are blind and cannot see. Help them to enjoy the shape and scent of the lovely things you have made. Amen.

Song   'This is the day'. *Come and Sing Some More*, Scripture Union.

3RD DAY BLUE

Have a display of blue objects. The children will probably need help to think of things that are always blue – the sea and sky on a sunny day, a bluebell, cornflower, sapphire. Some pictures would be useful. Show the children three jars of paint, one red, one yellow, one blue, and explain that we call them the primary colours. Other colours can be mixed from them. Let some children come to experiment (you will need extra jars and paper). Make green, orange and purple. Explain that we are fortunate having hands to paint pictures. Some people who have hands that don't work properly are very clever and learn to hold a paint brush between their teeth or toes.

Prayer Thank you, God, for crayons and paint. We like to make pictures and patterns with the lovely colours. Thank you for our hands to hold the pencils and brushes. Amen.

Song 'For all the strength we have'. *Someone's Singing, Lord*, A & C Black.

4TH DAY   GREEN

Have a green display.
One class beforehand could make a book about all the things they have thought of – grass, trees, plants, emerald, grasshopper, frog etc. This would be enjoyed by the other children.

Poem 'Green' by Moore in *Rhyme Time*, Hamlyn.
Talk to the children about how green is a restful colour; we can look at green trees and plants for a long time without becoming tired of it. Maybe that is why God made so much of it.

Prayer Lord, green is such a restful colour. Thank you for making the trees, leaves and the grass. We can look for a long time at these beautiful things in the countryside. Amen.

Song 'Over the earth is a mat of green'. *Someone's Singing, Lord*, A & C Black.

5TH DAY MORE UNUSUAL COLOURS

Read the poem 'It is grey out', Karla Kuskin, *Rhyme Time*, Hamlyn.

After a misty grey day we enjoy the bright colours even more.
Show the children a variety of objects to teach the names of some of the
more unusual colours, eg

    carrot – orange
    material or flower – mauve, purple, violet
    chocolate – brown
    soap – pink
    comb – turquoise

What a lot of different colours there are. God made people with different
coloured skins. Some people have dark brown skin if they come from a
hot country, some have yellow skin and some have pink skin.

Prayer   Thank you, God, that you made children with different coloured skins. Some of us have rich brown skins and some of
us have yellow skins and some of us are pink. Thank you that
you made us all and love us all. Amen.

Song   'He's got the whole world in his hands' (first two verses). *Sing
to God*, Scripture Union.

OR   'Jesus loves me'. *Hymns and Songs*, Ladybird Books.

Suggest that the children wear their favourite colour for the next
Assembly and be ready to sit with children wearing that colour.

6TH DAY   FAVOURITE COLOURS

Ask children to sit in groups according to the colour they are wearing.
Which colour is most popular? Suggest that the children make graphs
in their classrooms to show the class's favourite colour or to show
colour of eyes or hair etc.

Read poem 'What is pink?' Rossetti, *The Young Puffin Book of Verse*,
Penguin.

Discuss the colours of a rainbow with the children and sing together 'I
can sing a rainbow' in the book *Apusskidu*, A & C Black.

Prayer   We remember, heavenly Father, that you put a rainbow in the
sky to remind us of how much you love us. Thank you for
caring for us all the time. Amen.

OR   Prayer in *Lion Book of Bible Stories and Prayers*, Section 21.

Song   'God who made the earth'. *Sing to God*, Scripture Union.

7TH DAY CAMOUFLAGE

Show the children a polar bear cut out of white paper and a brown bear, cut out of brown paper. Explain to the children that brown bears live in forests and polar bears live in snowy places. Put the brown bear against a white piece of paper and then the polar bear. Which one shows up? Which one is hidden? Encourage the children to say why the polar bear is white – so that it cannot be seen easily; we call this camouflage. The book *Hide and Seek*, Oxford Scientific Films, Andre Deutsch has many useful pictures of animals using camouflage. Tell the children about the chameleon that can change colour to hide from his enemies. When it walks across brown earth it is brown and when it walks across grass it changes to green. The book *Danger Colours*, Oxford Scientific Films, Andre Deutsch, shows pictures of creatures that do not use camouflage but other means of protection.

Prayer Thank you, God, for all the creatures you have made: the ones with spots, the ones with stripes, creatures with patterns on their bodies or wings and those that can change colour. Amen.

Song 'If I were a butterfly'. *Come and Sing Some More*, Scripture Union.

Ask the children to think of things that are black *and* white for the next Assembly.

8TH DAY BLACK AND WHITE: ROAD SAFETY

Begin by showing one or two things that are *just* white, eg some flour or sugar, a piece of chalk; then one or two things that are *just* black, eg liquorice, a piece of coal. Then ask the children if they have thought of anything which is black *and* white. Have a bag of objects which you can produce one at a time as they are mentioned – eg dice, dominoes, model zebra, a model penguin. It is probable that there will be a piano in the room and you could point out the black and white keys.

Then produce a Zebra crossing made from paper and discuss its importance. Ask a few children to practise the kerb-drill with you. Other children could be the traffic. Encourage *all* the children to repeat the kerb drill at the end.

Prayer We thank you, God, for people who take care of us on the roads, for policemen and school crossing patrols. Help us to remember to be careful on the roads so that nobody gets hurt. Amen.

Song 'Come, let us remember the joys of the town'. *Someone's Singing, Lord*, A & C Black.

Books for follow-up work on colours – *Colour*, Macdonald Starters. *Colours of Things*, Althea, Dinosaur Publications.

Shapes

1ST DAY   SPIDER'S WEB

Show the children a picture of a spider's web and a picture of a spider, explaining how the spider makes its web with an almost invisible thread. Encourage the children to look at webs after the rain, when the sun is shining on them and making them sparkle. How wonderful that God designed such a beautiful pattern.

Show a lace mat and explain how it was made by a person using threads. People must have looked at God's pattern and tried to make something like it. They were copying God's design.

Prayer   Thank you, loving Father, for taking such care when you made our world. Thank you for all the interesting shapes and patterns and colours.

Song   'All things bright and beautiful'. *Come and Sing*, Scripture Union.

OR   'To God, who makes all lovely things'. *Someone's Singing, Lord*, A & C Black.

2ND DAY   PEACOCK'S TAIL

Show the children a picture of a peacock displaying its fan-shaped tail. Some of the children will have seen this and could express its beauty in language, written or spoken, also in paintings. Have one peacock's feather to show and look carefully at the 'eye' with its variety of blues and greens. Notice the way it shimmers as it moves in the light.

Show a fan to the children and explain how it was used in this country and still is used in other parts of the world to help a person to keep cool on a hot day. Someone must have seen God's design and copied it. The fan is the same shape as the peacock's tail.

Prayer   'And God saw everything that he had made and it was very good.' Father, we thank you for your world and everything in it that is beautiful and good. Help us to take care of all these good things. Amen.

Song   'This is a lovely world'. *Someone's Singing, Lord*, A & C Black.
OR   'I'm very glad of God'. *Someone's Singing, Lord*, A & C Black.

3RD DAY SPIRAL SHAPES

Show some spiral shapes that are man-made. This will depend on what is available – maybe a corkscrew or a picture of a helter-skelter. Some schools have spiral shapes included in their PE apparatus. With your finger show how a spiral shape starts at the top and goes round and round to the bottom. People made these spiral shapes, but I think God gave them the ideas. He designed many spiral shapes. Show the children some – eg a shell such as a whelk, a Scots pine cone, a bean plant growing round a stick, the seeds of a sunflower head. God let us share his ideas.

Prayer Thank you, Creator of the Earth, for making a world so full of interesting and exciting shapes. You took such care designing even the smallest shell and seeds. We praise you. Amen.

Song 'Praise him'. *Come and Sing*, Scripture Union.

4TH DAY LEAVES

Have a selection of leaves to show the children; a variety of shapes, large and small, wide and narrow, serrated and smooth edged, lobed etc. Discuss texture also; prickly, hairy, glossy. Look at the pattern made by the veins. Suggest that the children make some leaf rubbings or take leaf prints. Explain that in spring and summer the leaves are usually green and then many begin to turn brown and yellow in the autumn. The children could make a collection of different shaped leaves.

Poem 'Who has seen the wind?' by Christina Rossetti in *The Book of a Thousand Poems*, Evans.

Prayer Thank you, God, for tiny leaf buds. We love to watch them growing and we enjoy their colours and shapes. Thank you for the shade given by the leaves on a hot day and the rustling of the leaves as the wind passes by. Amen.

Song 'Over the earth is a mat of green'. *Someone's Singing, Lord*, A & C Black.

OR 'And God said'. *Come and Sing*, Scripture Union.

Helpful books are *Leaves from Trees*, Althea, Dinosaur, and *Guide to Trees*, Piccolo Explorer Book, Piper Books Ltd.

5TH DAY FINGERS

Ask the children to hold up one finger and look at the tip very carefully. Point out that they should be able to see a pattern of lines. Explain to the children that you are going to tell them something very wonderful. There are millions of people in the world, but every person has their own special pattern on their finger. Everyone has a different design; nobody has one just the same as you. God loves you so much that he made you with a special pattern of your own. Suggest the children try printing with the tips of their fingers and look at the patterns under a magnifying glass.

Prayer Thank you, Father God, for making me. Nobody is quite the same as me. You loved me so much that you made me in a very special way. Help me always to remember how much you love me. Amen.

Song 'If I were a butterfly'. *Come and Sing Some More*, Scripture Union.

OR 'He's got the whole wide world in his hands'. *Sing to God*, Scripture Union.

Useful books for the theme Shapes: *Discovering Everyday Things* and *Discovering Shapes and Designs* – both from Lion Publishing.

Pets

1ST DAY DOGS

If possible have a dog with its owner in Assembly and discuss what it looks like; short or long hair, shape of ears, size of tail etc and how it is cared for; needing somewhere warm and clean to sleep, the right sort of food, fresh water and exercise. One or two children could tell the others how they throw sticks or balls for their dogs to chase. Also stress that dogs need company and how, when we show kindness to them, they will usually be friendly towards us.

Children could show writing and drawings about their dogs. Read one or two of the following poems.

Poems 'My Puppy' by Aileen Fisher, *Young Puffin Book of Verse*
'Dogs' by Marchette Chute in *Rhyme Time*, Hamlyn
'Maggie' Anon in *Rhyme Time*, Hamlyn

Prayer Thank you, God, for friendly dogs that wag their tails and like to be near us. Thank you for all the fun we have with them. Help us to take good care of them. Amen.

Song 'Animal Sounds'. *Come and Sing*, Scripture Union (last verse about dogs).

Suitable follow-up stories are *Dinah the dog with a difference*, Scamp Series, Arnold & Son, and *Harry the dirty dog* by Gene Zion, Picture Puffin, Penguin.

2ND DAY CATS

If convenient have a cat with its owner in Assembly. Discuss the cat's fur, whiskers, claws, eyes etc and how it is able to keep itself clean by licking. Ask the owner how to care for a cat and keep it healthy. Explain that a baby cat is called a kitten. Younger children could sing 'I love little pussy' or 'Pussy cat, pussy cat'.

Poems 'Cat' by Mary Britton Miller in *Young Puffin Book of Verse*, Penguin Books.
'Cats' by Eleanor Farjeon in *Young Puffin Book of Verse*, Penguin Books.

Prayer Thank you, God, for cats. We like to watch them play as they creep silently and pounce suddenly. We like to touch their soft fur. Help us always to be gentle as we care for them. Amen.

Song   'Animal sounds'. *Come and Sing*, Scripture Union (4th verse about cats).

Suitable follow-up stories are *Millions of Cats* by Wanda Gag, Puffin Books in association with Faber & Faber. *The Outside Cat* by Jane Thayer, Knight, the paperback division of Brockhampton Press. *Catkin the Curious Kitten*, Scamp Series, Arnold & Son.

3RD DAY   RABBITS

A school rabbit or a visitor with a rabbit would be appropriate. Encourage the children to look carefully at the way it twitches its nose; at the long whiskers for feeling, the long ears and the short fluffy tail. If possible watch the way it moves. Discuss the rabbit's needs with its owner; the importance of clean straw in the hutch and fresh green food to eat.

Read one or two of the following poems. 'My new rabbit' by Elizabeth Gould in *Come Follow Me*, Evans. 'The Rabbit and the Fox' by Clive Sansom in *The Young Puffin Book of Verse*, Penguin Books. 'The Rabbit by Elizabeth Madox Roberts in *The Young Puffin Book of Verse*, Penguin Books. 'I had a penny', A A Milne in *When We Were Very Young*, Methuen & Co.

Prayer   Dear God, we thank you for rabbits so fluffy and soft, for the way they jump and then sit very still and listen with a twitching nose. Please help us to care for our rabbits and not forget to feed them and keep them clean.

Song   'All things bright and beautiful'. *Sing to God*, Scripture Union.

Suitable follow up story – *Peter Rabbit*, Beatrix Potter, Warne.

4TH DAY   GUINEA PIGS, HAMSTERS, GERBILS, MICE

These creatures could be brought into Assembly by children who own them and one at a time be taken out for everyone to see. Shape, size and colour could be compared and the teacher explain that they are all creatures called rodents, because they have special teeth for gnawing. The owners of these animals could describe how they care for them: cleaning the cages, finding out the right sort of food and showing the children the correct way of holding them.

Poem   'Mice' by Rose Fyleman in *Come Follow Me*, Evans Brothers.

Prayer Lord God, some of the creatures you made are very large –
the tall giraffe and the huge elephant. We are glad you made
some little creatures too, which we can hold and stroke.
Please give us hands that are gentle and kind. Amen.

Song 'Jesus' hands were kind hands'. *Someone's Singing, Lord*,
A & C Black.

Suitable follow-up stories. *Monty the runaway mouse*, Scamp Series,
Arnold & Son. *My class looks after pets*, Franklin Watts. *Hamster*, Stop
Watch Books, A & C Black. *Gerbils*, Junior Petkeepers Library, Franklin
Watts. *Guinea Pigs*, Petkeepers Library, Franklin Watts.

This series could be continued discussing other pets such as goldfish,
tortoise, budgerigar etc. It could end with a school pet show.

An Assembly series on farm or zoo animals could also be added, as
appropriate, linking with visits to a farm or zoo.

Seasons

Spring

1ST DAY FLOWERS

Take some of the most common spring flowers to Assembly and see how many the children can name – violet, primrose, wood anemone, daffodil, tulip. It may be possible to show bulbs in bowls planted by the children the previous autumn. Explain that bulbs outside flower early in the year because they have food stored.
Read the book *Flowers*, Althea, Life Cycle Books, Longman.

Prayer Thank you. God, for the spring flowers waking up after their winter rest. Thank you for their beautiful colours and shapes. Amen.

Song 'All the flowers are waking'. *Someone's Singing, Lord*, A & C Black.

OR 'The flowers that grow in the garden'. *Someone's Singing, Lord*, A & C Black.

2ND DAY TREES

Take some twigs into Assembly and look at the buds. Remind the children that many trees have been resting for the winter and are now beginning to grow again. Show willow catkins, called pussy willow because the catkins are hairy and soft like kittens' fur, and also leaf buds of the horse chestnut, called sticky buds because each leaf bud is covered with sticky shiny scales to protect it. Show hawthorn, explaining that some people call the flowers May blossom.

Prayer Thank you, God, for the springtime when the flowers and trees begin to grow again. We are growing too. Please help us to grow up into kind and useful people. Amen.

Song 'Sing a song of Maytime' (or springtime). *Hymns and Songs*, Ladybird Books.

OR 'Over the earth'. *Someone's Singing, Lord*, A & C Black.

3RD DAY BIRDS

Play a short part of a record or tape of bird songs. Explain that birds begin to sing again in springtime after the cold winter. They are very busy making nests too. Show one or two nests and look at the materials used. Discuss the different places birds choose to build their nests eg holes in trees, in a hedge, in the eaves etc. Establish that nests are for birds' eggs and how the parent birds take care of their young.

Prayer Thank you, God, for birds and their cheerful songs. Make *us* cheerful today, to show how glad we are to be in your world. Amen.

Song 'This is a lovely world'. *Someone's Singing, Lord*, A & C Black.
OR 'Thank you for the world so sweet'. *Hymns and Songs*, Ladybird Books.

4TH DAY THE FARMER

It would be helpful to have a toy harrow and drill on display. The farmer works hard in the springtime preparing the soil, ready to plant seeds. Explain that the earth is in big lumps and the farmer needs to break up the lumps before he can plant tiny seeds. Remind the children that their parents probably get soil ready in the garden too. Show the harrow used by the farmer to make the soil fine and smooth; also the drill, a machine which plants the seeds much more quickly than by hand. A selection of seeds such as oats, barley, wheat could be displayed somewhere in the school for the children to examine carefully later. Suggest they might like to grow seeds in their classroom – peas and beans in jam jars, cress on saucers etc.

Prayer Thank you, God, for the busy farmer sowing seeds in the springtime, so we can have food to eat later in the year.

Song 'The farmer comes to scatter the seed'. *Someone's Singing, Lord*, A & C Black.

5TH DAY   YOUNG CREATURES

This would be particularly appropriate after a visit to a farm. Spring is the time for baby animals to be born. Show pictures one by one and discuss names – lambs, piglets, foals, calves, ducklings, chickens. Discuss what they look like, the noises they make, how they feel when touched, how they are cared for etc.

Prayer   We thank you, God, for springtime when we think about new life. We thank you for the seeds growing and the buds bursting out into leaf and new creatures on the farms. Most of all we thank you for the Easter story telling us that Jesus is alive. Amen.

Song   'All things bright and beautiful'. *Come and Sing*, Scripture Union.

OR   'I'm very glad of God'. *Someone's Singing, Lord*, A & C Black.

OR   'Animal Sounds' (first three verses). *Come and Sing*, Scripture Union.

6TH DAY   SPRINGTIME IN THE PONDS AND STREAMS

This Assembly would be appropriate after children had been pond dipping or during the time they are watching tadpoles grow in their classrooms.
The book *Frogs*, Life Cycle Books, Althea, Longman, could be read Children who had been recording the development of the tadpoles could read their observations.
A useful poem is 'The Tadpole' by E E Gould in *Come Follow Me*, Evans.

Prayer   We thank you, Father God, for the fun we have looking in ponds and streams. We love to see creatures there; some that crawl, some that wriggle, others that dart about in the water partly hidden by the stones and weed. Thank you for all the interesting things you have made for us to enjoy.

Song   'And God said'. *Come and Sing*, Scripture Union.

Summer

1ST DAY   WORK OF THE FARMER

Remind the children of the work the farmer did in the spring – planting his seeds. Now the seeds have grown, because God has sent the sunshine and the rain. In some of his fields the farmer will have been growing grass and letting it grow taller and taller.

Remind the children that their parents probably cut the grass in the garden because they don't want it to grow tall. Point out that the farmer needs tall grass, because he cuts it down in the summer while it is still green to make silage for feeding his animals on the farm.

Later in the summer the corn is ready to be cut. Show the children a toy combine harvester and explain how it cuts the corn, threshes it and throws out the straw onto the field, while the seeds are dropped into sacks. The straw is usually pressed into bales by another machine.

The farmer is busy looking after his animals too. In summer time he shears his sheep – the woolly coat called a fleece is cut off in one piece. Stress that this in no way harms the sheep – it is rather like us having a haircut. If possible have a fleece for the children to see and touch.

Prayer   Thank you, God, for the work of the farmer looking after his animals and crops, so that we can have food to eat all the year round. Amen.

Song   'The farmer comes to scatter the seed',
OR   'When the corn is planted', both in *Someone's Singing, Lord*, A & C Black.

2ND DAY   SUMMER FLOWERS AND FRUITS

Have a display of summer flowers, soft fruits and vegetables grown for salads. Suggest to the children that next time they visit a local market, they might look out for these things. Markets are so colourful in the summertime, because there are many brightly-coloured flowers and fruits. Explain that many of these things are grown by people called market gardeners. A market gardener has very big greenhouses, which keep the plants warm. He usually has to water them every day – tomatoes, cucumbers, lettuces. The fruits – cherries, raspberries, strawberries, gooseberries, grow outside and need to be picked and put into little baskets called punnets. Suggest that each child might like to bring one flower from their garden (if they have one) and make a display – perhaps sorting them into colours or finding out their names and labelling them.

Prayer Thank you for summer, Father God, for bright red juicy strawberries, for curved green cucumbers, for pansies that feel like velvet. Thank you for the people who work hard to grow these things for us. Amen.

Song 'And God said'. *Come and Sing*, Scripture Union.

3RD DAY INSECTS AND BUGS

One class could bring pictures, paintings, models of insects they have found and observed, having looked under stones, on plants or in old sheds. Explain to the children that some insects are very useful, such as the ladybird, because it eats the little greenfly that spoils plants in the garden.

The honey bee is useful too because it gives us delicious honey to put on our bread and butter.

Some insects are very useful because they are a bit like a carpet sweeper! They eat up all the rubbish left on the ground and help to make our world tidy.

Some insects are very clever. Show a wasps' nest if one is available and let the children wonder at how the cells are made so perfectly from chewed wood – all the same shape and size.

Some insects are very beautiful, like the butterfly – its wings are made up of little scales that fit together (there is a good picture of this in *Discovering Everyday Things*, Lion Publishing). Each little scale is in exactly the right place to make up the beautiful colours and patterns we see. When a butterfly first hatches out, its wings are folded and crumpled but they dry out and then you can see their patterns.

Younger children would enjoy the book *The Very Hungry Caterpillar* by Eric Carle, Hamish Hamilton, and this would be more appropriate than a discussion about a variety of insects.

Prayer Thank you, God, for making such an interesting world for us to live in. We love to see the tiny spotted ladybird, the furry striped bee; the home of a wasp so carefully made and the fragile patterned wings of the butterfly. It reminds us how much you care for the world you have made. Amen.

Song 'I love God's tiny creatures'. *Someone's Singing, Lord*, A & C Black.

OR 'If I were a butterfly'. *Come and Sing Some More*, Scripture Union.

4TH DAY HOLIDAYS

Most children spend at least one day by the sea during a holiday period. A group of children could tell the others what they especially like to do – dig in the sand, paddle in the sea, look in the rock pools etc. An alternative would be for the children to mime these activities, so the others can guess. A large picture of a beach would be useful, and shells, sea urchins etc. Suggest to the children that during a holiday they might like to make a special collection eg shells, pebbles, pressed flowers. It should be pointed out that a collection could be made even if they just go out for one day eg tickets – for bus, entrance to zoo etc. Explain to the children that some things cannot be brought back from a holiday so they might like to draw them – live crab or starfish, sandcastle. Others could bring back postcards from museums or safari parks and mount them in scrap books.

Poems to read about the sea-side:
'There are big waves and little waves', Eleanor Farjeon, *Young Puffin Book of Verse*, Penguin Books.
'Until I saw the sea', Eleanor Farjeon, *Young Puffin Book of Verse*, Penguin Books.
'Pebbles', Edith King, *The Book of A Thousand Poems*, Evans.
There is enough material here for several days and parts can be selected to suit the particular children involved.

Prayer   Loving Father, thank you for days at the seaside, for running barefoot, digging in the sand, splashing in the water, exploring among the rocks. Thank you for the wonderful world you have made. Please bless boys and girls who never have holidays and have never seen the sea. Show us if there is something we can do to help them. Amen.

Song   'God made the shore'. *Come and Sing*, Scripture Union.

Autumn

1ST DAY SEEDS

A group of children could show pictures and patterns made with a variety of seeds. These can be glued to thick paper with PVC glue or into Polyfilla on a firm base. Establish that seeds are very important because plants grow from them. The children will probably have had experience of this, growing a variety of seeds in the springtime at school. Explain to the children that a flower or tree has seeds in the autumn and these seeds need to be scattered about so that new plants can grow. Show a dandelion seed head (dandelion clock) and ask a child to blow it like the wind. Suggest that the children look closely afterwards and see that each little seed is carried by a 'parachute'. The parachutes fly away and carry the seeds to a new piece of ground, so that new dandelions can grow. Other examples could be used eg sycamore wings.

Older infants would enjoy thinking of seeds we eat, or things that you eat which are made from seeds. Bread, cake and biscuits are made with flour which comes from inside the wheat, rye or barley seeds. We eat walnuts, hazelnuts and almonds. Peas, beans and lentils are seeds. Coffee and cocoa come from seeds. These older children might also enjoy the poem 'Seed Song' by Christopher Rowe in *Rhyme Time*, Hamlyn.

Prayer Father God, seeds are very tiny but they grow into beautiful flowers and tall trees. We are only small but we are growing too. Please help us to grow up into kind, useful people. Amen.

Song 'Be kind'. *Come and Sing*, Scripture Union.

OR 'God whose name is love'. *Hymns and Songs*, Ladybird Books.

2ND DAY HARVEST

Aim to show our thankfulness for God's gifts at harvest time. This theme could be approached in a variety of ways. A different aspect of harvest could be thought about each day for at least a week. The Assemblies about fruit, vegetables and cereal crops in the section on 'The Earth' and the 8th, 9th and 10th days under the section on 'Meals' would be useful. Also, this particular Assembly could be used in sections, although in its entirety it can be used for a special Harvest Service, to which parents are invited. Fruit, vegetables and cereal crops can be brought and displayed, then taken to needy people afterwards or alternatively the food sold after the service in order that the proceeds may be given to a charity eg Oxfam, Tear Fund.

Each class could make their contribution to the festival.

1) Fruit. A class graph could be held up to show which is the favourite fruit; the children having drawn theirs and placed it in the appropriate space.

2) Vegetables. Some children could show prints made with vegetables – potato, carrot etc. Vegetables could be placed in four sets to show that we eat some *roots* (potato, carrot, parsnip), some *stalks* (celery, leek), some *leaves* (cabbage, lettuce), some *flowers* (cauliflower).

Song 'See, here are red apples'. *Come and Sing*, Scripture Union.

3) Cereal crops. A class could show bread they have made and read or tell the other children how it was done. This could be followed by the poem 'Bread' by H E Wilkinson in *Come Follow Me*, Evans. Half the class say the first two lines in each verse and the other half say the second two lines. (The farmer could hold the corn, the miller hold a bag of flour, mother hold the loaf of bread.)

Song   'When the corn is planted'. *Someone's Singing, Lord*, A & C Black.

Prayers   We thank you, heavenly Father, for all your gifts to us at Harvest time; for fruit and vegetables, for the ripe corn, for all our food and the farmers who grow it for us. Amen.
Loving Father God, we remember that some people in other countries do not have enough to eat. Please help the leaders of our country to find ways of sharing our food, so that no one needs to be hungry. Amen.

4) A song to mime (suitable for the younger children),
'We are going to plant a bean' in *This Little Puffin*, Puffin Books.
This is the story of a plant growing. You may prefer to alter the words slightly.
1st verse We are going to plant a bean
2nd verse Then the summer sun will shine
3rd verse Then the little bean will grow
4th verse Then we pick the beans to eat

5) The tale of a turnip
A class could act the story. Characters needed according to the version.
Helen Oxenbury – old man, old woman, grand-daughter, black dog, cat, mouse.
Ladybird – old man, old woman, boy, girl, dog, cat, mouse.
The rest of the class could join in the repetitive parts – 'they pulled and they pulled'. Percussion may be added eg xylophone (low to high) each time they pull, with the addition of one beat on a cymbal when the turnip eventually comes out of the ground.

Song   'Thank you for the world so sweet'. *Hymns and Songs*, Ladybird Books.
OR   'For health and strength and daily food', *Sing to God*, Scripture Union.
The leader of the assembly ends with a verse from Psalm 67
'The land has produced its harvest; God, our God has blessed us.'
The book *Thank you for a loaf of bread*, Lion Publishing, if not already used, would link well with the Harvest theme.

3RD DAY PREPARING FOR WINTER

Explain to the children that when autumn arrives, we start to prepare for the colder weather. Suggestions may come from the children – we buy warm winter clothes, adults bottle fruit while there is plenty of it and make meals to put in the freezer ready for the time when we have no fresh vegetables etc.

The birds and animals need to get ready for the colder weather too. A group of children show the others what happens.

1st child speaks: 'I am a swallow. I fly away to a warmer country.' (Child uses arms as wings and flies away)

2nd child speaks: 'I am a dormouse. I curl up in a ball and go to sleep.' (Child curls up on floor)

3rd child speaks: 'I am a squirrel. I am collecting nuts and hiding them so I can eat them during the cold winter.' (Child pretends to hide nuts in the ground)

4th child speaks: 'I am a toad. I am catching flies now before I go deep down in the mud at the bottom of the pond.' (Child jumps on hands and feet and then stays very still)

The words hibernation and migration could be explained.

Prayer Thank you, God, for my Mum and Dad helping to get me ready for wintertime. Thank you for strong new shoes and warm coats and gloves. Thank you for caring for the animals and birds too, as they get ready for winter.
We are glad that you care for all the creatures you have made. Amen.

Song 'God takes good care of me each day'. (first two verses) *Come and Sing*, Scripture Union.

Winter

1ST DAY RAIN

A child could stand at the front wearing waterproof clothes, wellington boots and holding an umbrella. Ask what sort of weather the child is dressed for.

Poem 'Happiness', A A Milne, *Rhyme Time*, Hamlyn.
Sometimes we have just a little light rain called drizzle, or a short time of rain called a shower. Sometimes it rains and rains all day and you can hear it pattering on the roof and watch it trickling down the window panes.

Poem 'Rain Sizes', John Ciardi, *Rhyme Time*, Hamlyn.
Some people don't like the rain because they can't go out or because they get very wet, but rain is very precious. It is very useful – why? Encourage the children to give reasons – water for drinking, to make the trees and flowers grow etc. Where does the rain come from? Explain it comes from the clouds. (A few older infants will be interested to know how it gets into the clouds. Water from lakes and seas rises and collects in the air; when the cloud is cooled and becomes heavy with moisture it rains.)

Prayer Thank you, Father God, for the rain giving us water to drink. Thank you for the rain falling on the trees and flowers to make them grow. I like my waterproof clothes that keep me dry and the fun I have splashing in the puddles. Please help me not to grumble if I can't go out to play. Amen.

Song 'Down the air'. *Hymns and Songs*, Ladybird Books.
OR 'I love the sun' (one verse about the rain). *Come and Sing*, Scripture Union.

2ND DAY WIND

Show a picture of a windy day. What sort of a day is this? How do you know it is windy? The answers will depend on the pictures – the trees are swaying, papers are blowing about, someone's hat has blown off etc. Blow on your hand and make a little wind. Can you feel it? – Can you see it? We cannot see the wind but we can feel it and we can see what the wind does by looking at the pictures.
Poem 'Who has seen the wind?' Rossetti, *Book of a Thousand Poems*, Evans.
We cannot see the wind, but we know it is there. We cannot see God but we know he is everywhere.
Sometimes the wind is gentle and we call it a breeze, sometimes it is very strong and we call it a gale. These two poems are about a strong wind.
'Go Wind' by Lilian Moore, *Rhyme Time*, Hamlyn.
'Windy Nights' by Rodney Bennett, *Rhyme Time*, Hamlyn.
Wind is very useful. What does it do? Encourage the children to give suggestions – eg it dries clothes, it carries seeds to new places, it moves sailing boats.

Prayer Thank you, God, for the fun of windy days when we can fly our kites and sail our boats.

Please take care of people in very windy places – the fishermen out at sea and the lifeboatmen who help people in rough weather. Amen.

Song   'And God said'. *Come and Sing*, Scripture Union.
'I can't see the wind'. *Come and Sing*, Scripture Union.

3RD DAY SNOW

This Assembly would obviously be best during or after a period of snowy weather. The children could bring pictures and writing about the things they like to do on a snowy day; build a snowman, ride on a sledge, make snowballs etc.

Explain to the children how, when it is very cold, the drops of water falling from the clouds are turned to tiny pieces of ice. These very tiny pieces join together to make snowflakes and a snowflake always has six points. We can see these under a microscope. Every snowflake is different, just as people are different, but they are all beautiful. Think about how beautiful the world looks on a snowy day – everywhere looks white and clean; how the snow rests on twigs and gates; the fun of being the first person to walk across a stretch of snow; how the world seems very quiet and still.

Although most children enjoy snow, there are some old people who find it makes life difficult. Encourage the children to think of ways to help those people eg make a slide in their own garden, rather than on the pavement where an old person might slip and hurt themselves.

Poems   'Winter Morning' by Ogden Nash, *Young Puffin Book of Verse*, Penguin Books.
'The North Wind', *The Book of a Thousand Poems*, Evans.

Prayer   Dear God, we thank you for the snow which makes our world so beautiful. Thank you for the fun we have playing in it and for our warm homes and hot dinners on a cold day. Amen.

Song   'To God who makes all lovely things' verses 1 and 3. *Someone's Singing, Lord*, A & C Black.

OR   'I love the sun'. *Come and Sing*, Scripture Union. Make up a new verse –
            I love the snow
            It falls on me.

4TH DAY   FROST

Some days in winter it is very cold. We need to wear our warm clothes. One child could be dressed suitably with coat, hat, scarf, gloves. We need to switch on our central heating or light fires at home and our School Caretaker makes sure our school is warm too. Sometimes there is a frost at night and it makes the grass white and the playground slippery. Sometimes frost makes lovely patterns on our windows and the twigs outside look as if they are covered in sugar.

Poem   'Jack Frost' by Cecily E Pike, *The Book of A Thousand Poems*, Evans.

We are well and strong and can run about to keep warm on a cold day. Some children are going to show you a game to play on a frosty day – 'Here we go round the mulberry bush' with actions, found in *This Little Puffin*, Puffin Books.

Prayer   We thank you, loving Father God, for cold and frosty mornings. Thank you for making us well and strong so we can run about to keep warm. Amen.

Song   'For all the strength we have'. *Someone's Singing, Lord*, A & C Black.

OR   'For health and strength and daily food'. *Sing to God*, Scripture Union.

5TH DAY   BIRDS IN WINTER TIME

We have been thinking about the cold weather in winter. Mummy or Daddy make sure you are wearing your warm clothes and they usually make you a hot dinner or tea to warm you up. Mummy and Daddy can still go shopping to buy food for you. But the birds find winter a difficult time. On warm sunny days the birds find insects and berries and seeds to eat, but in the winter they can't find these things. So, kind people help to feed the birds in wintertime. Show some pictures of birds the children might see – robin, tit, thrush, blackbird, sparrow. Show a picture of a bird table and some food that children might put on it; crumbs of bread, seeds in a bag to hang up, bacon rind. Birds need water too in the wintertime, so you might put out a dish of water. Why can't birds get water from the ponds and puddles in very cold weather? Talk about water freezing.

Poem   'Tea with me' by Alison Winn, *The Young Puffin Book of Verse*, Penguin Books.

Prayer Thank you, loving Father, that you take care of me every day. Thank you for the birds. Please help us to take care of them, especially in the wintertime. Amen.

Song 'Little birds in winter time'. *Someone's Singing, Lord*, A & C Black.

Useful books on the theme Seasons –
The Nature Table series by Trevor Terry and Margaret Linton, *Spring, Summer, Autumn, Winter*, Evans.
The Snowy Day by Ezra Jack Keats, Penguin Books in association with The Bodley Head.
The Four Seasons, Parramon editions, Fountain Press Ltd.

Festivals

Christmas

1ST DAY   PREPARATION FOR THE CHRISTMAS STORY

Invite a mother and baby to Assembly and discuss how the mother and father prepared for the baby and about the loving home waiting for the baby to come. Ask the mother what sort of things had to be made, borrowed or bought – clothes, somewhere for the baby to sleep, a baby bath etc. Encourage the children to say how they think the mother cares for the baby – making sure he is warm enough, keeping him clean, feeding him. Stress how important it is too for the baby to have interesting things to look at, eg mobiles and toys to play with; but most of all the baby needs to be loved and cuddled and hear his mother's voice.
Explain to the children that you are going to tell them a story, which will last for several days, about a very special baby and how his mother got ready for him.

Prayer   Thank you, loving Father, for all the babies I know. Please help their Mummies and Daddies to look after them well. Thank you for this little baby. We pray that he/she will grow up knowing your love. Amen.

Ask the children to sing quietly so as not to frighten the baby.
Song   'Lullaby Jesus'. *Carol Gaily Carol*, A & C Black.
Explain that a lullaby is a special song for babies to help them to sleep. Suggest some children might make books about babies and the things they need, using pictures from catalogues and magazines.

2ND DAY   THE ANGEL VISITS MARY

Bible story   Luke chapter 1, verses 26–38
Start by discussing the way we send messages to people if we can't speak to them ourselves – use the 'phone, write a letter etc. Explain that God wanted to send a message and used a very special way to do it. He doesn't usually send us messages like that now. He sent an Angel to give the message.
Mary lived in Nazareth in a little white house with a flat roof. Tell the

children some of the things she did to look after her home – brushed floor, brought water from the well etc. She loved God very much and wanted to please him. There was a man called Joseph in the village and Mary and Joseph became friends and they liked each other so much they decided to get engaged. One day Mary was in her home – you could suggest what she was doing – perhaps sitting sewing – when suddenly a bright light filled the room and Mary realised there was someone standing beside her. She felt frightened at first, then a voice said, 'Do not be afraid, Mary', and Mary looked up and there was an Angel beside her. The Angel said – 'I have come to bring you good news, Mary. You are going to have a baby. He will be a very special baby because he will be God's Son. You must call him Jesus.' Mary said, 'Let it be just as you say.' Then the Angel went away and the room became dark again and Mary felt so excited and so pleased that she had been chosen to be the mother of God's baby son. She said a special thank you prayer to God.

We are going to say a special thank you prayer too.

Prayer Thank you, God, for all mothers everywhere. Thank you for my mother who looked after me when I was a tiny baby. Thank you for choosing Mary to look after baby Jesus. Amen.

Song 'I can't see the wind'. *Come and Sing*, Scripture Union.

3RD DAY   MARY VISITS ELIZABETH

Bible story   Luke chapter 1, verses 39–56

Who has a best friend? Is it nice sharing secrets with your friend? Sometimes special things happen at home and you can't wait to get to school so that you can tell your friends – we like to share news, don't we? Do you remember that Mary had some special news – what was it? – Yes, she was going to be the mother of baby Jesus. She wanted to tell her friend Elizabeth so she hurried there right away. Mary said, 'I am going to be the mother of God's Son – my baby will be called Jesus.' Elizabeth was so pleased and said, 'I have some news too – I am going to have a baby too and my baby will be called John'. Then Mary sang a special song to God because she was so happy. She stayed with Elizabeth for three months and then went back to her own home in Nazareth to wait for her baby.

Prayer We praise you, God, just like Mary and Elizabeth did so long ago. We praise you because you sent baby Jesus to earth to an ordinary home just like ours. Bless our homes today and make them happy places because we love you. Amen.

Song 'Praise him'. *Come and Sing*, Scripture Union.

4TH DAY   PREPARATIONS FOR THE BABY

Do you remember the baby who came to school and all the things his/her mummy got ready? Mary and Joseph had to get things ready too. Joseph was a carpenter so he might have made a wooden cradle for the baby and some wooden toys. Mary would make some clothes for the baby – not like our babies wear – a piece of material like a big bandage that she would wrap him in – called a swaddling band (demonstrate with a wide bandage around a doll). Let any children whose mothers are expecting babies show books they have made of pictures from magazines showing prams, bottles etc.

Prayer   We have heard about Mary and Joseph getting their home ready for baby Jesus. Lord, please bless my mother and father and all those who take care of me. Make me obedient, kind and helpful in my home. Amen.

There are suitable prayers also in *Prayers for everyone* and *Prayers for Home and School* – Little Lions, Lion Publishing.

Song   'He's got the whole wide world in his hands'. *Sing to God*, Scripture Union.

OR   'God takes good care of me each day'. *Come and Sing*, Scripture Union.

5TH DAY   JOURNEY TO BETHLEHEM

Bible story   Luke chapter 2, verses 1–7

One day a messenger came to Nazareth to tell everyone that they were going to be counted – a census – people had to go back to the town where their families came from. Joseph had to go back to a city called Bethlehem. Mary would go with him – I expect she took some of the baby things with her in case the baby came while she was away. They probably went on a donkey because the journey would take several days and they would camp out each night – sleeping under the stars. When they reached Bethlehem the city was very crowded and they tried to find somewhere to stay. Mary was very tired because the time was coming for her baby to be born. All the inns (like hotels but you cooked your own food) were full. At last one kind innkeeper said, 'I have no room in my inn but you can sleep in the stable if you like.' Mary and Joseph were very grateful and went into the stable with the animals and lay down in the hay.

Prayer   We remember today the kind innkeeper who made room in his stable for Mary and Joseph. Lord, there are many grown-ups and children today, all round the world, who have nowhere to live. Some do not have enough food and clothes. Some are ill. Please show us ways of helping them. Amen.

Song   'Be kind'. *Come and Sing*, Scripture Union.

OR   'Little donkey'. *Carol Gaily Carol*, A & C Black.

6TH DAY BIRTH IN THE STABLE

Do you remember where Mary and Joseph had to sleep? Yes, in a stable with the animals – oxen, donkey, cows, etc. Joseph made a soft bed for Mary in the hay and that night a very wonderful thing happened – baby Jesus was born. Mary wrapped him up in swaddling clothes and put him in the manger – the trough that the animals fed from. Mary and Joseph knew that God had sent his Son into the world and they both said 'thank you'. That was the very first Christmas. If it is possible to have a crib scene (the olive wood figures from Israel are ideal) this could be gradually built up during the story – putting in the animals first, and the manger, then Mary and Joseph and lastly the baby Jesus. A cardboard box on its side with hay in it, would be perfectly suitable for the stable, if a more permanent one is not available.

Prayer   Thank you, God, for sending Jesus to be born in a stable on the first Christmas Day. Amen.

OR   God our Father, we love to have presents on Christmas Day. Help us to remember that Jesus is the best present of all, given to the world on the first Christmas Day. Amen.

Song   'Jesus our brother, kind and good'. *Carol Gaily Carol*, A & C Black.

OR   'Away in a manger'. *Merrily to Bethlehem*, A & C Black.

OR   'Jesus, Baby Jesus'. *Come and Sing*, Scripture Union.

7TH DAY SHEPHERDS

Bible story Luke chapter 2, verses 8–20

Talk about the life lived by shepherds – looking after sheep – using sling and crook. Walked in front of sheep to guide them. At night lit fire to keep wild animals away – wrapped themselves in cloaks to keep warm. One would guard sheep while others slept. One night shepherds near Bethlehem were guarding sheep as usual when suddenly the sky became very bright and they saw an angel. At first the shepherds were very frightened because they had never seen an angel before and the light was very bright. But the angel said, 'Don't be afraid. I have come to tell you some wonderful news. Jesus has been born tonight in Bethlehem. You will find him wrapped up in swaddling clothes in a manger.' Then the angel was joined by many more angels all singing together and praising God. Then gradually the light faded away and the angels went back to heaven. The shepherds said, 'Come on, let's go to Bethlehem and see this wonderful new baby.' I expect they left one shepherd to guard the sheep and maybe they took a lamb with them to give baby Jesus for a present. They knew that they must look in a stable because the angel said that Jesus was in a manger. They crept to the door and peeped in and Mary smiled and asked them to come inside. They looked at the new baby and they thanked God for sending him. Then they hurried away and told everyone they met about the wonderful things that had happened that night.

Prayer Lord God, it is wonderful that you chose poor men to be the first people to visit baby Jesus. Thank you that the shepherds wanted everyone to know the good news. Help me to let other people know about Jesus too. Amen.

Song 'Wind through the olive trees'. *Carol Gaily Carol*, A & C Black.
OR 'Merrily to Bethlehem'. *Merrily to Bethlehem*, A & C Black.
OR 'It was on a starry night'. *Merrily to Bethlehem*, A & C Black.

8TH DAY WISE MEN

Bible story Matthew chapter 2
Do you know what an astronomer does? He studies the stars – he needs to be a very clever person. At the time that Jesus was born there were some clever men who knew all about the stars. One night when they were studying the sky they saw a new star which they had never seen before – they knew it meant that a new king had been born. They said, 'Let's go and see the new king and take him presents.' One took gold, the others took frankincense and myrrh, which are things that have a lovely perfume. They travelled for a long, long time, following the star at night and resting by day. If you were looking for a king, where would you look? In a palace, of course, so the Wise Men went to Jerusalem and asked where they could find the new king. When King Herod heard, he was very cross – 'I am the king – there is no other king.' So he asked his special helpers to look up in their books and find out where a new king was to be born. They said, 'In Bethlehem.' So King Herod sent for the Wise Men and said, 'Go and look for the child in Bethlehem and when you have found him come back and tell me so I

can go and visit him too.' He did not really want to worship the new king – he wanted to hurt him. So the Wise Men set off again and the star shone over a house in Bethlehem. Mary and Joseph and baby Jesus were living in a house there now – the Wise Men had been a long time coming to find him. They went inside and knelt down and gave Jesus their gifts – gold, frankincense and myrrh. Then they returned to their own land. They didn't go back through Jerusalem because God told them in a dream to go home a different way, so King Herod couldn't harm Jesus.

Prayer   Thank you, God, for showing the Wise Men the way to Jesus. We cannot bring expensive presents like the Wise Men but we bring our love to Jesus today. Amen.

Song   'Follow the star.' BBC Watch record.

OR   'Jesus, Baby Jesus'. *Come and Sing*, Scripture Union.

The set of pictures called 'The Nativity', E J Arnold, is particularly suitable for infant-aged children.

Easter

1ST DAY PALM SUNDAY

Bible story   Matthew chapter 21, verses 1–11; Mark chapter 11, verses 1–11

Ask one child to wear a crown. Who wears a crown? – a king or queen. A king is a very important person; we like to see him and wave flags. We like to please him and obey him especially if he is a good king. I am going to tell you a story about a special king. (Show a toy donkey or a picture of one and explain that a donkey comes into the story too.)

One day Jesus and his friends were going to the big city of Jerusalem; they were walking in the hot sun and Jesus said to two of his friends, 'Go to a nearby village and you will find a mother donkey and a young donkey tied to a post; untie the young donkey and bring it to me. If anyone says, "What are you doing?", say "I need to borrow the donkey." The man who owns the donkey won't mind.' I expect Jesus knew him. The friends of Jesus went to the village and found the young donkey. They said, 'Jesus needs him.' The owner was very kind and said of course Jesus could borrow the donkey – he knew Jesus would take care of it and bring it back. The friends of Jesus put their coats on the donkey's back to make it nice and comfortable for Jesus. Then Jesus rode on the donkey into the city. A lot of people saw him coming.

They had no flags, so they broke down some branches from the trees and waved them, cheered and shouted out 'Praise King Jesus.' It was a very happy day. Many people remembered how Jesus had been kind to their little children, made sick people better and helped those who were sad or lonely. All those people who loved Jesus called him their King. If we love Jesus we shall want to do what he asks us to do and we shall want to make him glad. We shall want to call Jesus our King too.

Prayer   We praise you, Lord Jesus, that you are a very special sort of King. Help us always to obey you and to love you. Amen.

Song   'Praise King Jesus'. *Come and Sing*, Scripture Union.

OR   'We have a King who rides a donkey'. *Someone's Singing, Lord*, A & C Black.

OR   'Praise him, praise him'. *Come and Sing*, Scripture Union.

2ND DAY THE DEATH AND RESURRECTION OF JESUS

Bible story   John chapter 20, verses 1–18

Remind the children of the Palm Sunday story.

Many people loved Jesus because he was always good, kind and gentle; but there were some people who did not like it when the people cheered and waved the branches. They felt jealous because they wanted to be the most important people in the city. They felt cross and they sent some soldiers to find Jesus and take him as a prisoner; but Jesus hadn't done anything wrong. The soldiers took Jesus to a hill. They laughed at him and made him a pretend crown of prickly leaves and then they killed him – it was *very* sad – but do you remember that Jesus is a very special sort of King? So something special is going to happen. The friends of Jesus put his body in a cave in a beautiful garden and lots of strong men rolled a big stone in front of the cave. That day was a Friday. All Friday and Saturday the friends of Jesus were very sad because he was dead. They remembered all the kind things he had done – how he had blessed little children, stopped the big storm, made the sick boy better, made friends with a lonely little man. They remembered all the lovely stories he told. They thought, 'We'll never see him again – he was our very best friend.'

On the Sunday morning there was a friend of Jesus called Mary (not his mother, another Mary) – she was very sad too and went into the beautiful garden and found that the big stone had been rolled away from the cave. She was very surprised and wondered who could have moved the stone. She looked into the cave. Inside there were two angels. They said, 'Do not be afraid. Jesus is not here. He has come alive again.' Mary couldn't believe it. She still felt sad and had tears in her eyes. Someone in the garden said, 'What are you crying for?' Mary thought it was the gardener and she said, 'I am sad because Jesus has gone.' Then the voice said just one word, 'Mary.' At once she recognised the voice of Jesus – she looked up and saw him. Oh how glad she was. They talked together in the beautiful garden and Jesus said to her, 'Tell all my friends that I am alive.' So Mary ran quickly to tell his friends, 'He is alive, I have seen Jesus in the garden.' What a wonderful day that was. It was the first Easter Day.

Prayer   Thank you, God, for the message of Easter. We thank you that Jesus is alive for evermore. Amen.

Song   'Praise King Jesus'. *Come and Sing*, Scripture Union. Second verse is about resurrection.

OR   'King Jesus is risen'.

OR   'Mary, Mary, why are you sad?' Both from *Come and Sing Some More*, Scripture Union.

3RD DAY   TWO FRIENDS ON THE JOURNEY TO EMMAUS

Bible story   Mark chapter 16, verse 12; Luke chapter 24, verse 13
Aim to show the sadness and disappointment of Cleopas and his friend as they walk together, how a stranger joins them and accepts their offer of hospitality. Stress the joy the two men have as they realise it is Jesus and how they hurry back to Jerusalem to tell their friends that Jesus is alive again.
This story may be found in the book *Jesus is alive*, Bible Societies.

Prayer   Thank you, Lord Jesus, for showing your friends that you are alive for always. Please be with me in my work and play, at home and at school. May I grow more like you day by day and show other people that you are my friend. Amen.

Song   'Jesus is the best friend'. *Come and Sing*, Scripture Union.

Whitsun

Tell a story about a family at home one day – father, mother and children. Father was using his electric drill in the shed, mother ironing, John using his electric train set. Suddenly Dad's drill stopped working, the iron stopped working and the train stopped on the track – why? – because there was a power cut. No power, so no work. In just the same way we need power if we want to do God's work and please him – we need God's power called the Holy Spirit. At Whitsun we remember that God gave his power, his Holy Spirit, so we can use his power to do his work.

Tell stories of people who have used God's power, Dr Barnardo, Florence Nightingale, Gladys Aylward etc. Most books are written for older children but the following give facts which can be adapted for infants.

Faith in Action Series – The Religious Education Press

A Home for All Children (Dr Barnardo)

Helen (Helen Keller)

Friend of Prisoners (Elizabeth Fry)

Florence Nightingale, Elizabeth Fry, Ladybird

Heroes of the Cross, Marshalls

Songs 'I want to work for Jesus'. *Come and Sing*, Scripture Union.
'Hands to work'. *Someone's Singing, Lord*, A & C Black.
'God is pleased when we are friends'. *Come and Sing Some More*, Scripture Union.
'Who can see the great wind blow' (for older infants only). *Someone's Singing Lord*, A & C Black.

Prayers (to be used when appropriate)
Thank you, God, for people who have worked hard to make other people happy. Thank you for making them brave and kind. Please help me to be like that too. Amen.

Dear God, we try to please you, but it is sometimes very hard. Please give us your power so we can do the right things. Amen.

Father God, we cannot see your Holy Spirit, but we know that he helps us and comforts us and teaches us about you. Thank you for your special power for us to use each day. Amen.

The Bible

1ST DAY   THE BIBLE

Put out a display of Bibles, making sure that some look really attractive. It would be good to have some that marked a particular celebration, also maybe an old one, as well as a modern colourful Children's Bible with pictures. Explain to the children that the stories inside are all the same, although the outside covers look different. Stress that they *all* say how much Jesus loves them and they tell us what sort of a person Jesus wants us to be. There are also many exciting stories.

We can go into almost any bookshop and there will be Bibles for sale, but in our country a long time ago and today in many places of the world people can't buy Bibles easily. We are very happy that we can buy Bibles in many shops.

Tomorrow I am going to tell you a story about a little girl who wanted a Bible. She had to work very hard to get one.

Prayer   Thank you, God, for all the Bibles in our country. Thank you for the stories I hear about you and your love for me. May children all round the world hear of your love for them too. Amen.

Song   'How do I know that God loves me?' *Come and Sing*, Scripture Union.

2ND DAY   THE STORY OF MARY JONES, PART 1

Tell the children this is a true story. Useful visual aids are a slate, a candle and a Bible for this first part of the story.

Mary Jones was a little Welsh girl – 200 years ago she lived in a big village in Wales, surrounded by mountains. She lived with her Mummy and Daddy in a little stone cottage. They were very poor. Her Daddy was a weaver (remind children what this means) and her Mummy had lots of jobs to do – washing, baking, mending. Daddy sold the woollen things he made and Mummy got money for doing mending for other people. There were no taps with water, but a little stream outside their house where they washed themselves and their clothes. There was no light to switch on – they had a candle. Near their cottage was a ruined castle on a hill – still there – Mary used to play there and pretend she was a princess. Mary did not go to school because there were no schools near her house – so she could not read or write, and her Mummy and Daddy couldn't either. Mary used to go to church with her Mummy and Daddy – they heard there how much God loved them. The man at the chapel used to read to them out of a big Bible. A Bible is like this – full of stories of how God loves us – we can't see him – but he is caring for us all the time. Mary thought, 'I wish I could read the Bible, but I can't go to school to learn how to read.' One day as they were coming out of the little chapel they met Mrs Evans, a farmer's wife – she said, 'Did you like the story today, Mary ?' and Mary said, 'Oh yes, I wish I could read and then I could read all the lovely stories in the Bible.' Mrs Evans said, 'Mary, if you ever learn to read you can come to my house to read our Bible.' Not many people had Bibles because they cost a lot of money in those days. All the way home Mary threw up piles of leaves because she was so happy and sang, 'I will learn to read. I will learn to read. I am sure God will help me to learn to read.' One day something wonderful happened – Daddy came home and he said there was going to be a school in a village not too far away and Mary could go if she liked. She was *so* pleased but then said, 'Who will help you, Mummy?' Mummy said, 'Don't worry, I'll manage. We want you to go to school to learn to read and write.' The day arrived and Mary washed in the stream, waved goodbye and jumped over the stones by the river. She passed the castle where she used to play and walked by the river to school. She prayed, 'Please God, teach me to learn to read so I can read the Bible.' There were lots of other children at the school and they had a nice teacher called Mr Ellis. He gave all the children a slate and they began to learn the letters just like you do. Mary listened very hard to the teacher and found she could make the letters quite easily, so she helped the other children who found it hard. At dinnertime the children had brought their own food – bread and cheese and after they had eaten it they ran about before school in the afternoon. Mary worked hard every day and soon she could read a lot of words and write some too. She thought, 'Perhaps soon I shall be able to read the Bible'. (Tomorrow we'll see if she does.)

Prayer   Father God, we thank you for books to read and enjoy and for our teachers at school who teach us to read and write. Thank you for our Bibles and the people who read the stories to us.

3RD DAY   THE STORY OF MARY JONES, PART 2

Do you remember how Mary Jones had started going to school and was learning to read and write? Do you remember how a kind farmer's wife, Mrs Evans, had said Mary could come to the farm to read their big Bible? Next time she saw Mrs Evans she said, 'Have you remembered you said I could come? I can read some words now.' Mrs Evans was very pleased and said, 'Come any time you like.' She set off one day to the farm and Mrs Evans let her in and gave her a lovely Welsh cake to eat. Then she showed Mary where she kept the Bible – on a table by the window. Mary had to stand up to read because she wasn't very tall and the table was quite high. She found one of her favourite stories about a sheep that got lost and how the shepherd found it. Often Mary used to go to the farm to read – she couldn't manage all the words but she could read some of them.

Mary still went to school during the week, and one day she came home and said, 'Mummy, there is going to be a special school on Sundays to learn about Jesus – can I go?' Mummy and Daddy said 'Yes'. She loved the special Sunday school and wished she had a Bible of her own so she could read the stories whenever she liked. Well, one day, Mary was washing some clothes in the river by their house when she suddenly had a wonderful idea. 'I could save up money to buy my own Bible' – and she began to sing, 'A Bible for me, a Bible for me.' So she ran inside to tell Mummy and Daddy. Mummy said, 'But Mary, there aren't any Bibles in Wales for us to buy and they cost such a lot of money anyway.' Daddy said, 'I'm sure it is a good idea – I'll make you a little box to put the money in that you save.'

Then Mummy had an idea – 'Mary, you have some hens – you could sell the eggs and get some money. You could do some mending for people or weed their gardens.' Mary was very excited and began to save. One person asked her to look after her little children and she did this so well that they gave her some money. She sold some of her eggs and she did mending and weeding – do you know she had to save for years and years, not just a week or a month or one year, but for a very, very long time.

One day she found a purse with lots of money in it, but she didn't keep it, she found who it belonged to and gave it back. The man was so pleased he gave her a coin out of it.

When it was Mary's birthday her Mummy and Daddy made her a lovely woollen shawl because she had worked so hard saving her money. One day Daddy said he had heard about a man called Mr Charles who lived at Bala, 25 miles away, and Daddy said Mr Charles had some Bibles to sell – only a few left. So Mary worked even harder until at last she had enough money. She said – Now I will walk to Bala to buy my Bible – at last I have enough money, and she thanked God for all the people who had helped her to save.

There were lots of kind people who had helped her.

(Tomorrow we'll hear about Mary going to fetch her Bible.)

Prayer   Thank you, God, for all the kind people who helped Mary in the story. Thank you for the people who help me and make me happy. Please show me ways of being kind to someone else today. Amen.

4TH DAY THE STORY OF MARY JONES, PART 3

A knapsack would be useful as a visual aid.

Do you remember Mary Jones had saved up enough money for a Bible? – she had saved for years and years. Do you remember there was a man at Bala 25 miles away who had some for sale? So at last one day Mary said, 'Tomorrow I shall go to Bala.' 25 miles is a *very* long way – much further than you walking to school, much further than you walking to (give example). It would take a whole day to walk there. So Mummy got some sandwiches ready and put them in a knapsack, and Mary put the money in it. When Mary got up she got dressed and splashed her face in the stream and waved goodbye. She knew the first bit of the journey because she had walked that way before – past the hill with the ruined castle and then she began to climb up a steep hill. She didn't see anyone, just the sheep, but she knew God was taking care of her. The sheep had marks on their backs to show who they belonged to. At last she came to a village. A lady said, 'Where are you going?' Mary said, 'To get a Bible.' The lady gave her some milk to drink. Then Mary walked on and she began to feel hungry so she stopped to eat some sandwiches from her knapsack. She made sure the money was safe. The sun was hot so she tied a hanky round her head and walked on. At last she came to a little cottage and another kind lady gave her some milk to drink, and water to wash her face. Her feet ached now because she had walked so far. 'I am going to get a Bible,' she said. 'Go that way to Bala,' said the lady. At last she came to a little town – 'I think this must be Bala,' said Mary – but a lady said, 'No, this is not Bala, you must walk right to the other end of the lake.' She was very tired but she hurried on as it was getting near night time. She asked some people where she could find Mr Charles and they said, 'He will be in bed now, but you could stay the night with us.' They were very kind. Mary woke early the next morning and felt under her pillow for the money – yes, it was safe. She washed and dressed and put on her boots and went to find the house where Mr Charles lived. He was surprised to find a little girl coming to visit him. 'Where have you come from?' 'All the way over the mountains.' 'What have you come for?' 'To buy a Bible,' said Mary. 'But they cost a lot of money,' said Mr Charles. 'Yes, I know, but I have been saving for years and years,' said Mary. Then Mr Charles looked very sad. 'Oh dear, I have got three Bibles but I have promised them to other people.' Mary thought of how long she had waited and began to cry. Then Mr Charles said, 'I can't let you go home without one – have this one, someone else won't mind waiting.' 'Oh, thank you,' said Mary. Then Mary and Mr Charles said a prayer to God – 'Thank you for Mary coming all this way – thank you for the Bible.' Then he gave Mary a drink in the kitchen and Mary put the Bible in her knapsack. A kind man said he would take Mary part of the way home in his cart pulled by a horse. Then Mary walked the rest of the way singing, 'My Bible, my Bible.' She reached home safely and often read the wonderful stories about how much Jesus loves us.

Prayer   Lord Jesus, thank you for all the stories in the Bible telling us how much you love us. We are glad that we can buy Bibles in our shops. Please teach us new and wonderful things. Amen.

Songs for this theme
'God wants us to obey him'. *Come and Sing,* Scripture Union.
'Jesus loves me'. *Hymns and Songs*, Ladybird Books.

Prayer

1ST DAY   JESUS IS NEVER TOO BUSY TO LISTEN

Philip is a boy about the same age as you. He finds writing very difficult, but one day his teacher at school said, 'Philip, what lovely writing.' His teacher was very pleased because he had tried so hard. Philip was *so* pleased and wanted everyone to know about his lovely writing. On the way home from school he saw his friend Julia. Philip was just going to tell her about his writing when Julia said, 'I can't stop. I'm going swimming.' Never mind, thought Philip. I'll go straight home and tell Mum. He ran up the path – 'Mum, Mum, guess what happened at school today.' 'Not now, dear,' said Mummy. 'I'm just getting the baby some tea.' Philip felt a bit sad and waited for Dad to come home. 'Dad, do you know what—' 'Not just now, Philip, I've got an important letter to finish,' said Daddy. Philip so wanted someone to listen and later on Mummy and Daddy did listen and were very pleased. I know sometimes your teachers are busy and you have to wait for help. Sometimes Mum and Dad are busy and you have to wait. It is very hard to wait. *But* there is one person who is *never too busy* to listen and I'm going to tell you a story about that person.
The story may be found in *Storytime 1*, page 79, Scripture Union. Matthew chapter 19, verses 13–15, Blessing the Little Children. Aim to show the children's disappointment at being turned away and their joy when Jesus called them to him.

Prayer   Thank you, Lord Jesus, that you are never too busy to listen and that you always love me and my friends. Amen.
Song   'Jesus is the best friend'. *Come and Sing*, Scripture Union.
A child could read 'God always listens' from *Hymns and Songs*, Ladybird Books, to finish the Assembly.

2ND DAY   JESUS LISTENS TO PRAYER AND ANSWERS PRAYER

The Friend at Midnight. Luke chapter 11, verses 5–10.
I know a little boy who wanted a rabbit and his Mummy said, 'You can only have one if you remember to feed it every day.' 'Oh yes,' said the little boy. 'But will you keep on looking after it?' said Mummy. 'It is hard to *keep things up* every day.' Are you good at *keeping things up*? When

your teacher asks you to keep the books tidy in your classroom *all* week, do you remember the job for two days and then forget and not *keep it up*? Sometimes we remember to pray to Jesus – we say thank you for my nice warm home and please look after my friend in hospital and then we forget to *keep it up* and we stop talking to him.

Jesus doesn't want us to give up praying. The answer isn't always 'Yes' if we are asking for something because sometimes we ask for things that wouldn't be good for us. Sometimes Jesus says 'No' or 'Wait' just like your Mummy or teacher does.

Jesus told a story about someone who didn't give up. There was once a man who liked having visitors. He always made them welcome – I expect you do too. You probably help to get ready for your visitors, make them a specially nice tea and watch Mummy put clean sheets on the bed. But this man did not know he was going to have a visitor. He was just going to bed one night when a visitor called at his house; it was very late and the visitor had travelled a long way. The man didn't know his friend was coming, so it was a lovely surprise – but of course he hadn't got anything ready! 'Come in and sit down. I'll get you something to eat. You must be hungry and thirsty after your journey.' So the man went to get his friend some food – but oh dear he had run out of bread. He only had a tiny bit left. 'Never mind,' he said, 'I'll go next door and see if my next door neighbour could let me have some.' You remember it was very late, don't you, and when the man went round to his neighbour's house, he found all the family had gone to bed. There wasn't any answer when he knocked at the door, so the man knocked again. Then he heard a sleepy voice. 'Who is that? What do you want? I'm in bed!' 'Please, can you help me?' said the man. 'I have a visitor and I can't make him a nice meal because I have no bread. Could you let me have some, please?' 'I'm in bed,' shouted the neighbour, 'and the children are asleep. I can't get up now.' The man felt disappointed so he knocked again. 'I'm sorry to bother you, but I do so want to give my friend something to eat – please help me.' At last the neighbour in bed decided to get up and find some bread. It was very kind of him and luckily he had some bread to share. The man was very glad and hurried back home and cooked a lovely supper for his visitor and they enjoyed being together again.

Jesus said we should be like the man in the story and *keep things up*. When we ask Jesus for something we should *keep on asking* until we get an answer. Don't forget that the answer is sometimes 'Yes', sometimes 'No' and sometimes 'Wait'. Jesus wants us to have the very best things he can give us.

Prayer Dear Lord Jesus, sometimes I start to pray for my friends and then I give up. Please show me the right things to ask for. Help me to keep on asking until my prayer is answered. Thank you that you always want the very best for everyone. Amen.

Song 'God always listens whenever we pray'. *Hymns and Songs*, Ladybird Books.

OR 'God hears and answers'. *Come and Sing*, Scripture Union.

3RD DAY   WE NEED TO TALK TO JESUS

The story of Martha and Mary. Luke chapter 10, verses 38–42.
This may be found in *Storytime 1*, page 67, Scripture Union.

Prayer Lord Jesus, sometimes I am very busy working at school, playing with friends, helping Mum and Dad at home. Don't let me forget to talk to you. Amen.

Song 'Heavenly Father, hear my prayer'. *Hymns and Songs*, Ladybird Books.

OR 'Talking to God'. *Come and Sing*, Scripture Union.

4TH DAY   WE NEED TO LISTEN TO JESUS

The story of Samuel

Bible story   1 Samuel chapter 3
This may be found in 'God speaks to Samuel', *The Lion Story Bible*, Book 16, Lion Publishing.

Prayer Lord Jesus, I can't hear your voice like I hear my friends talking to me. But sometimes you put good ideas into my mind and help me to think of kind things to do. No one else can hear what you put into my mind. Thank you for having that special way of talking to me. Amen.

Song 'God is pleased when we are friends'. *Come and Sing Some More*, Scripture Union.

OR 'I'm very glad of God'. *Someone's Singing, Lord*, A & C Black.

5TH DAY   WE SHOULD PRAY EVEN WHEN IT IS HARD

Daniel in the Lions' Den

Bible story   Daniel chapter 6

This story may be found in the book *Storytime 2*, page 34, Scripture Union.

Prayer   Lord Jesus, please make me brave, so that I do and say the right things even when it is hard. Thank you for taking care of Daniel. Thank you for taking care of me too. Help me to talk to you even when my friends think I am silly and tease me. Amen.

Song   'No, never alone'. *Sing to God*, Scripture Union.

OR   'Jesus is the best friend'. *Come and Sing*, Scripture Union.
A verse could be added
'Jesus is the best friend
I know that he loves me
He helps me when I feel afraid
I'm glad that he loves me.'

Jesus the helper

Joy

1ST DAY   WHAT MAKES US HAPPY?

Opening verse:–
To God who makes all lovely things
How happy must our praises be
Each day a new surprise he brings
To make us glad his world to see
Children sing 'If you're happy and you know it, clap your hands' in
Apusskidu, A & C Black.
One class show a book they have made of 'Things we enjoy' – this will
probably include such things as riding my bike, going out to tea with
Granny, playing by the sea etc. God gives us all the things that make us
happy, so we should say thank you.

Prayer   Thank you, God, for all the things that make us happy. May
we think of ways of making other people happy too.

Song   'This is a lovely world'. *Someone's Singing, Lord*, A & C Black.

OR   'Oh, how good is the Lord'. *Come and Sing Some More*,
Scripture Union.

2ND DAY   MORE HAPPY THINGS

Listen to some cheerful music. Read the book *Happiness is a warm
puppy* by Charles Schulz, Attica Publications (leaving out any part that
is not suitable for your particular children). Suggest that the children
make their own book called 'Happiness is –'.

Prayer   Dear God, our Father, we thank you for all your love for us; for
our families and friends, for our homes, our food and our
clothes and for the beautiful world you have made. Amen.
Any of the prayers in *Thank you for the world*, Little Lions, would be
suitable also.

Song   'Thank you Lord'. *Come and Sing Some More*, Scripture
Union.

OR   'Thank you for the world so sweet'. *Hymns and Songs*, Ladybird Books.

3RD DAY THE STORY OF THE TEN LEPERS

Bible story Luke chapter 17, verses 11–19
Introduction I expect most of you can remember our School Christmas party. One year the children in my class had a lovely time; they played games and they had a delicious tea. At the end of the party the Mummies and Daddies came to take them home and all the children ran off laughing and telling their families about the fun at the party. Then suddenly the door opened again and one child came back – I wonder what he came back for? He came to say thank you for a lovely party. That did make me pleased. I wonder if you remember to say thank you? I am going to tell you a story today about someone who remembered to say thank you.
This story can be found in *Storytime 2*, page 73, Scripture Union. Aim to show the sadness of the ten men, their joy at being healed and how Jesus especially was pleased because one man remembered to say thank you.

Prayer Ask the children what they would especially like to say thank you for and use their ideas in a prayer.
Lord Jesus, thank you for –.
Some of the older children might like to read thank you prayers from *The Lion Book of Children's Prayers*, Lion Publishing.
Song 'Thank you, Lord, for this fine day'. *Come and Sing Some More*, Scripture Union.
OR 'Praise him'. *Come and Sing*, Scripture Union.

Sadness

1ST DAY CHILDREN SHARE THEIR EXPERIENCES OF SADNESS

One class show their pictures and writing about sad things – these will probably include such ideas as pets dying, illness on the day of a party etc. Explain to the children that Jesus knows when we are sad or disappointed and it says in the Bible that he even knows when a little sparrow falls to the ground.

Prayer Lord Jesus, you know when we are feeling very sad. Help us to remember that you are always with us. Amen.
OR The first prayer on page 20 of *The Lion Book of Children's Prayers* beginning 'Lord Jesus, I pray for those who will be unhappy today'.

Song 'Jesus the best friend' (first verse). *Come and Sing*, Scripture Union.

OR 'God who made the earth'. *Sing to God*, Scripture Union.

2ND DAY   HOW CAN WE HELP SAD PEOPLE?

Explain to the children that there are many sad people and encourage them to think of ways they can help. Make sure these are really within the children's capabilities. You may need to give a few ideas eg if a new child at our school is crying in the playground or in the corridor what would you do? (Ask the child to join your game or show them where they want to go.) if you know an old or sick person who can never go out what could you do? (Draw a picture and take it to them or write a letter to cheer them up.) Suggest they join in 'Blue Peter' appeals if appropriate.

Prayer Dear Lord Jesus, help me to remember what it feels like to be sad and help me to think of ways to make other people happy. Amen.

The prayer called 'Unhappy children' in *Prayers for everyone*, Little Lions, is suitable.

Song 'Hands to work and feet to run'. *Come and Sing*, Scripture Union.

OR 'Be kind'. *Come and Sing*, Scripture Union.

3RD DAY   BLESSING THE LITTLE CHILDREN

Bible story Matthew chapter 19, verses 13–15
This story may be found in *Storytime 1*, page 79, Scripture Union. It is called 'Jesus and the children'. Aim to show the sadness of the children as they were turned away and their joy when Jesus called them back.
Other suitable Bible stories are
Jesus and the Little Girl, Bible Societies.
Jairus' daughter, *Storytime 2*, page 57, Scripture Union.

Prayer Lord Jesus, thank you that you are never too busy. You always have time to listen to me and to help me. Make me remember that you always love me and know what is best for me. Amen.

Song 'Let the children come'. *Come and Sing*, Scripture Union.
OR 'In Galilee beside the sea'. *Come and Sing*, Scripture Union.

Loneliness

1ST DAY   WHAT WE LIKE TO DO WITH OUR FRIENDS

Play music, 'Nimrod' (one section, from Enigma Variations) and explain to the children how Elgar wrote music about his friends.
Ask the children what they like to do with their friends – play games, share secrets etc. Suggest that they write a description of a friend, paint a portrait of a friend, or measure a friend.
How lovely it is to have friends.

Prayer   Please join in 'We thank you, God' after each line.
For eyes to see our friends –
For voices to speak to them –
For ears to hear our friends –
For all the fun we have with our friends –
For Jesus, the friend of everyone –. Amen.
There are some prayers on the theme of 'Our Friends' on page 34 and page 35 in *The Lion Book of Children's Prayers*, Lion Publishing.
Song   'In Galilee beside the sea'. *Come and Sing*, Scripture Union.

2ND DAY   PEOPLE WHO HAVE NO FRIENDS

Ask the children if they have ever felt lonely – you may need to explain what the word means. We feel sad and lonely when we have no friends or think no one cares about us. Encourage the children to think about people who might be lonely in their village or town or at school. What do you think a girl might feel like if she came to our school and she didn't know any of the children and no one asked her to play with them? What could you do? What do you think a boy might feel like if he moved into your road or street from another town and he saw children playing out on their bikes and kicking balls but he didn't know any of their names? What could you do? What do you think a child feels like when he or she comes from another country to our town? The people might have different coloured skins and eat different food and everything seems strange. What could you do?

Prayer Lord Jesus, it is not nice to feel lonely. Please help me to make friends with other children, especially those who are new at our school or new in our street or who come from another country. Please help me to play kindly, to share and to say I'm sorry when I spoil a game, so I can be friends again. Amen.

Song 'Be kind'. *Come and Sing*, Scripture Union.

OR 'Father we thank you for the night'. *Someone's Singing, Lord*, A & C Black.

3RD DAY   PEOPLE WHO ARE LONELY IN THEIR WORK

Ask the children to think of people who may be lonely in their work because they are a long way from their families or friends. Some children could show pictures of these people or read their writing about the jobs these people do eg lighthouse keeper, astronaut, soldiers away from home. They all do important jobs.

Prayer We thank you, loving Father, for people who work in lonely places –
– for fishermen, lighthouse keepers and men on oil rigs
– for policemen walking round the streets at night
– for nurses on night duty when everything is quiet
– for divers and astronauts
May they know your help and comfort when they are lonely. Amen.

Song 'Hands to work and feet to run'. *Someone's Singing, Lord*, A & C Black.

4TH DAY   ZACCHAEUS THE LONELY MAN

Bible story Luke chapter 19
Aim to show that Jesus knew Zacchaeus was lonely and how he made friends with him.
The story may be found in *Storytime 1*, page 87, Scripture Union, or it can be acted by a group of children.

Prayer Lord Jesus, we are glad you want to be friends with everyone. Thank you for loving us even when we are grumpy or greedy or unkind. Help us to be sorry. Thank you that you still want to be our friend. Amen.

Song 'For the things that I've done wrong'. *Come and Sing*, Scripture Union.

OR 'Jesus is the best friend'. *Come and Sing*, Scripture Union. Second and third verses are particularly appropriate.

Fear

1ST DAY CHILDREN SHARE FEARS

The children show pictures and their own writing about things that make them afraid (this will probably include such things as big animals, night-time, getting lost etc). Tell them that Jesus said, 'I am with you always.'

Prayer Lord Jesus, sometimes we are frightened when we get lost or when we are in the dark. Help us to be brave and may we remember that you are caring for us all the time. Amen.

Song 'I need not be afraid'. *Come and Sing Some More*, Scripture Union.

2ND DAY PEOPLE WHO HELP US WHEN WE ARE AFRAID

Play some music that suggests fear eg part of 'The Planets', Holst. Remind the children that they thought yesterday about being afraid. Explain to them that there are many people who will help them when they are afraid, their parents, their teachers, policemen or policewomen. Stress the fact that policemen are our friends who will help us if we are lost or worried.

Prayer Thank you, Lord, for the people who help us when we are frightened, for policemen who protect us, for Mummy and Daddy who are there to comfort us and most of all for your care for us every day. Amen.

Song 'Jesus the best friend'. *Come and Sing*, Scripture Union. A new verse could be added – 'He helps me when I feel afraid'.

OR 'God who made the earth'. *Sing to God*, Scripture Union.

3RD DAY THE STORM ON THE LAKE

Bible story   Mark chapter 4, verses 35–41
This story may be found in *Storytime 1*, page 75, Scripture Union. Aim to show that Jesus helped his friends when they were afraid.

Prayer   Lord Jesus, we are glad you helped your friends in the storm. Please bless people today who are feeling afraid and show them that you are with them always. Amen.
Some prayers on page 30 of *The Lion Book of Children's Prayers* are suitable.

Song   'Peter's brown boat'. *Come and Sing*, Scripture Union.
OR   'God takes good care of me'. *Come and Sing*, Scripture Union (first two verses).

Sickness

1ST DAY

Children share experiences of illness and visits by the doctor. A group of children could show their pictures and read accounts of times they felt ill. Encourage other children to express how they feel when they are ill – sometimes very hot, tired, not wanting food, not wanting to play, wanting a grown-up near you etc. What happens when Mum and Dad can't help you to feel better? Whom do we call? Discuss the doctor coming to visit and how he decides what sort of medicine would be best. A group or class of children sing 'Miss Polly had a dolly who was sick, sick, sick' in *Okki-tokki-unga*, A & C Black. Two children could mime the doctor and Miss Polly.

Prayer   Dear Father God, I am glad I have a friendly doctor who sees me at his surgery or clinic – or comes to see me in bed at home when I feel too ill to get up. Please help my doctor to do his work well, especially when he is very busy. Amen.

Song   'For health and strength and daily food'. *Sing to God*, Scripture Union.

Suggest that children who have nurses' or doctors' dressing-up clothes wear them for the next Assembly.

2ND DAY HOSPITALS

Explain to the children that sometimes our family doctor knows we need special care to make us well again and he decides we need to go to hospital. Talk about doctors and nurses in hospital, drawing on the children's experiences. Introduce words such as wards, ambulance, stethoscope, temperature, pulse, injection etc. Stress that although Mum and Dad might have to go home, they will visit regularly.

Prayer We are well and strong. Thank you, Lord. We pray for people who are in hospital. Thank you for giving the doctors and nurses clever minds to know how to make ill people well again. Thank you for their gentle hands too. Amen.

Song 'For all the strength we have'. *Someone's Singing, Lord*, A & C Black.

The book *Going into Hospital*, Althea, Dinosaur Publications, may be useful.

3RD DAY THE CENTURION'S SERVANT

Bible story Luke chapter 7, verses 1–10.
Aim to show the love of Jesus for those who are ill and his healing power. The Centurion's Servant can be found in *Storytime 2*, page 64, Scripture Union.

Prayer Lord Jesus, the boy in the story did not see you, but you helped him. I cannot see you, but I know you will help me too. Thank you. Amen

Song 'Jesus' hands were kind hands'. *Come and Sing*, Scripture Union.

Being the sort of person Jesus wants me to be

1ST DAY   KIND

Tell the story of The Good Samaritan, Luke chapter 10, verses 30–35. This story may be found in *Storytime 1*, page 71, Scripture Union, or *The Good Samaritan*, The Bible Societies.

Prayer   Thank you, Lord Jesus, for the people who are kind to me. Please help me to think of kind things to do for other people, not just for my friends, but for everyone I meet. I want to have fun playing, without being rough or unkind. Make my hands gentle hands like yours, and help me to speak kind words too.

Song   'Be kind'. *Come and Sing*, Scripture Union.

OR   'God, whose name is Love'. *Hymns and Songs*, Ladybird Books.

2ND DAY   A GOOD FRIEND

Bible story   The paralytic healed, Luke chapter 5, verses 18–26
This story may be found in *Storytime 1*, page 83, Scripture Union.

Prayer   Lord Jesus, I am so glad I have friends. Please help me to be a good friend. Help me to keep promises, share my toys and play games fairly without cheating. Help me to be patient when other children are slow or don't know what to do, to be friendly with children who are shy and to look out for those who have no one to play with.

Song   'God is pleased when we are friends'. First 2 verses. *Come and Sing Some More*, Scripture Union.

OR   'Kum ba yah' 5th verse in *Sing to God*, Scripture Union.

3RD DAY   UNSELFISH

Bible story   Abraham and Lot, Genesis chapter 13, verses 5–11
This story may be found in *Storytime 1*, page 13, Scripture Union. You will probably need to discuss 'choosing' first. When a friend comes to tea and there are little cakes or biscuits, each one different, do you take the one *you* want first or do you let your friend choose first? It is hard to let someone choose first, isn't it? The story is about someone who remembered to do that.

Prayer   Lord Jesus, sometimes I want to choose the best thing for myself. Next time I am playing with my friends, please help me to let them choose the game. When there are special cakes or biscuits for tea help me not to want first choice. Please help me to be unselfish, and think about what other people would like. I know that is the sort of person you want me to be. Amen.

Song   'Father we thank you for the night'. *Someone's Singing, Lord*, A & C Black.

4TH DAY   SOMEONE WHO SHARES

Bible story   Feeding of the five thousand, John chapter 6, verses 1–14
This story may be found in *Storytime 2*, page 68, Scripture Union. It is called 'Sharing a picnic.'

Prayer   Jesus, please help me to share my toys and books and not just to keep them for myself. I know that is what you want me to do. Amen.

Song   'All that I have'. Sing to God, Scripture Union.
OR   'I want to work for Jesus'. Come and Sing, Scripture Union.

5TH DAY   HONEST

Bible story   Matthew the cheat
This story may be found in *Storytime 1*, page 58, Scripture Union. The words honest and dishonest will probably not be understood. Explain that the man in the story was dishonest or a cheat because he took

things that did not belong to him. When he had met Jesus he wanted to be honest. He didn't want to take other people's things.

Prayer   Lord Jesus, please help me to be honest. Help me to remember to give back things I have borrowed from other children. If I find something I like very much help me to remember to give it to a grown-up person, so they can find who it really belongs to. I know that is what you want me to do. Amen.

Song   'For the things that I've done wrong'. *Come and Sing*, Scripture Union.

6TH DAY   BRAVE

Bible story   David and Goliath, 1 Samuel chapter 17
This story may be found in *Storytime 2*, page 21, Scripture Union. If you have no sling available, you will need a picture of one, and discuss how it was used.

Prayer   Jesus, sometimes I feel scared. Then I remember you are stronger than anything or anyone. You love me and will take care of me. Help me to be brave when I have to do difficult things. Amen.

Song   'Only a boy named David'. *Singalong Songs*, Marshall, Morgan & Scott.

OR   'Jesus is the best friend'. *Come and Sing*, Scripture Union. (Make up a new verse 'He helps me when I feel afraid.')

7TH DAY   OBEDIENT

Bible story   Joshua and Jericho, Joshua chapter 6
Have you ever seen a town or city with walls built round it – thick, strong walls of stone built a long time ago to keep enemies out? We don't need towns with walls round now, because all the people in our country are friends.

A very long time ago some people who loved God had travelled a long way to find a new country that God was going to give them to live in. When they had nearly reached the new land they found a big city with thick walls round it. It was called the city of Jericho. The people who loved God were worried. 'We can't get into our new country. We can't fight the people in Jericho, because they are very safe, shut up in their strong city.'

The leader of the people, who loved God, was called Joshua and he said to his army, 'We must do just what God says.' God told Joshua his plan; it was a *very* strange one. Joshua said to his army, 'God says all our soldiers must march round the city of Jericho once every day for six days. In front the people who teach us about God (called the priests) have to blow horns (like a trumpet) but everyone else has to be very, very quiet; they must not say a word. On the seventh day we must march round the city seven times and then we have to make a very big noise. The priests will blow the horns and everyone must shout. Then the walls of the city will fall down flat and we can walk straight in.'

I expect all Joshua's men thought that was a very silly idea, but they were sensible because they knew that God's plan is always best. The people in Jericho thought it was very strange too when they saw all Joshua's army lining up and walking round the city on the first day. I expect the people in Jericho laughed and shouted rude things. Joshua's army did the same thing for 1, 2, 3, 4, 5, 6 days but on the seventh day, when the soldiers had walked round the city seven times, the priests blew their horns and the army made a great big shout – thousands of people making as much noise as they could – what a noise that would be!

Suddenly the walls of Jericho began to crack and crumble and fell down with an enormous crash. Then Joshua's men walked into the city just like God had told them to do.

What a good thing they did as God said. God always knows best. His plans are the best, so it is sensible to obey them.

Prayer   Dear Father God, sometimes I do not like to do what I am told. Please help me to obey my parents and teachers. Thank you that your plans are always best. Please help me to obey you. Amen.

Song   'Quickly obey'. *Come and Sing*, Scripture Union.

8TH DAY   USEFUL

Bible story   Palm Sunday, Mark chapter 11, verses 1–11
This story is told from the donkey's point of view.

The Little Donkey

I wonder if you have ever ridden on a donkey; maybe at the seaside? That is a lovely thing to do. The donkeys have such soft grey coats and they like you to stroke them.

Long ago in the land where Jesus lived many people rode on donkeys. The very rich people, who had a lot of money, rode on horses or camels, but the ordinary people rode on donkeys if they were travelling somewhere.

This is a story about a very special donkey. He was only a young donkey and he lived with his mother donkey in a field. Mother donkey carried things on her back; baskets and bundles. Sometimes she carried people on her back too. She was a very kind mother donkey and took great care of her baby. She was always there to help him when he was tired or afraid. Little donkey snuggled up to his mother and felt very safe. Most days little donkey was very frisky. That means he liked to run about in the field and kick up his heels. He always did just what he wanted.

One day he was tied up with mother donkey outside the house where his master lived. Two men came along the road and began to undo the rope that tied the little donkey to the house. The donkey's owner said, 'What are you doing with my donkey? The two men said 'Our friend Jesus needs the donkey – can we borrow him for a little while and we'll bring him safely back? Jesus will take great care of him.' 'Of course Jesus can borrow my donkey,' said the owner and he gave the men the rope, so that they could lead the donkey away. Off they went along the road, clippety clop, clippety clop. The little donkey was very frisky; he jumped about all over the place and he kicked up his heels. It must have been very difficult to lead him along the road. Soon they came to a group of men and one of them was Jesus. The two men said, 'This donkey is very frisky. I don't think anyone has ridden him before.' Jesus went up to the little donkey and stroked his nose. Little donkey thought that Jesus had such a kind face and he decided he would like to help Jesus. Jesus put his cloak across the donkey's back to make a saddle and the little donkey did not mind at all. He stayed very still and he didn't kick up his heels. Then Jesus climbed onto the donkey's back. It was the first time he had ever carried anyone, but he didn't mind. Off they went down the road to the big city of Jerusalem. The people there were so pleased to see Jesus. They clapped and cheered and some people put their coats in the road, so the donkey felt as if he was walking on the grass in his field. Some children waved branches from the palm trees and shouted, 'Hurrah, hurrah', because they were so pleased to see Jesus. The little donkey was not afraid, because Jesus was very gentle. The little donkey behaved beautifully. When Jesus got down from his back he said, 'Thank you little donkey; you *have* helped me today.' Then the friends of Jesus took the donkey back to his master and he went back into his field. He felt very happy because he had carried Jesus so carefully. He was glad he had been such a useful donkey.

Prayer   Dear Lord Jesus, thank you for using the little donkey. Please make me useful too. Help me to think of ways of helping other people today. Amen.

Song   'Donkey story'. *Come and Sing Some More*, Scripture Union.

9TH DAY   HELPFUL

Bible story   Ruth and Naomi, Ruth chapters 1, 2, 3, 4
This story may be found in *Storytime 2*, page 17, Scripture Union.
After the story the children could think of ways they could help other people.

Prayer   Jesus, show me something helpful I can do. Give me good ideas of ways to help my family – wiping the dishes or setting the table. I want to be a good helper at school too, taking messages for the teachers and tidying the classroom. We can show our love for you by helping other people. Please make me a cheerful helper today. Amen.

Song   'Hands to work and feet to run'. *Come and Sing*, Scripture Union.

10TH DAY   GENEROUS

Bible story   The widow's offering, Mark chapter 12, verses 41–44
This story may be found in *Bible Storytime*, Book 2, International Bible Reading Association, called 'A poor woman's gift'. At the end of the story it will be necessary to help the children apply it to themselves – the fact that a little gift bought with their own money is more special than an expensive gift paid for by their parents etc. If a number of children go to Sunday School they could be reminded that they might give one or two little coins which they have saved up themselves. That would make Jesus glad.

Prayer   Thank you, Lord Jesus, for my pocket money and the coins given to me by kind Aunties and Uncles. I like to buy sweets and toys. Please help me to save some of my own money to be kind to someone else and make them happy. Amen.

Song   'Two little fishes'. *Sing to God*, Scripture Union. (The second verse is appropriate.)

OR   'I want to work for Jesus'. *Come and Sing*, Scripture Union.

11TH DAY   MAKING VISITORS WELCOME

Bible story   Elisha and the Shunammite woman, 2 Kings chapter 4, verses 8–10

Making visitors welcome (Elisha)

I wonder if you sometimes have visitors in your house? Perhaps Mummy lets you have a friend to tea and I expect she says, 'Let your friend choose a cake first because he is a visitor.' We want visitors to feel happy in our home. Perhaps someone comes to stay for a night; maybe Granny or a friend. I wonder if you have to share a bedroom with your brothers or sisters so there is room for the visitor? I'm sure you don't grumble about it, because you want the visitor to feel happy and comfortable. Sometimes you are especially glad because a visitor comes to stay from another country. Maybe you have been to stay with someone else and your friends have tried hard to make you happy and give you the things you like to eat and share their toys or take you out to interesting places, so you enjoy yourself.

I am going to tell you a story about a lady who welcomed a visitor into her house.

There was once a lady who used to look out of her house, and often saw a traveller going by. He used to go about helping people and telling them about God. His name was Elisha. When the lady saw him she thought, 'I wonder if he is hungry. He won't know anyone in our town. I have plenty of food and could ask him in for dinner.' Elisha was very pleased and said thank you to the kind lady. She asked him to come again and that's just what happened. Every time Elisha came to the town where the kind lady lived he called to see her and her husband and they all had dinner together. Elisha stayed a few days in the town and told the people about God and helped them. The kind lady wondered where Elisha slept at night-time because he didn't have a house in that town. She thought he might just sleep on the ground somewhere, which must have been very uncomfortable. So the kind lady and her husband had a very good idea. They decided to make Elisha a special little room of his own at the top of their house. Soon it was made and the kind lady put a bed in it and all the other things she thought Elisha would need; a table, a chair and a lamp. Next time Elisha came he found a special little room for himself and the kind lady said, 'You can stay here every time you come to our town to tell people about God.' They became very good friends, all because the lady had been so kind and thoughtful to a visitor in her town.

Prayer   Dear God, please help us to make our homes happy places where visitors always feel welcome. Help us to look after our visitors well and always to be friendly and kind to them for Jesus' sake. Amen.

Song   'Be kind'. *Come and Sing*, Scripture Union.

12TH DAY   CARING ABOUT PEOPLE WHO ARE BAD OR SAD OR LONELY OR COME FROM A DIFFERENT COUNTRY

Bible story   Naaman and the servant girl, 2 Kings chapter 5. This story may be found in *Storytime 2*, page 30, Scripture Union.
Other suitable stories are Zacchaeus (page 110), The Good Samaritan (page 114), Matthew (page 115). The woman at the well (John chapter 4, verses 4–42, selected parts).

Prayer   Thank you, Lord Jesus, for your love for everyone. Thank you for caring about bad people. Thank you for caring about sad or lonely people. Thank you for caring about people who come from different countries. Your love is very wonderful. Please help me to care about all these people too. Amen.

Song   'We have a king'. *Someone's Singing, Lord*, A & C Black. Verse three 'We have a king who cares for people' is appropriate.

OR   'Jesus loves me'. *Hymns and Songs*, Ladybird Books.

13TH DAY   LEARNING NOT TO BE JEALOUS

Bible story   Joseph and his brothers, Genesis chapter 37
I wonder if you sometimes feel jealous or rather cross if your brother or sister has something new or special and you wish you had it. Maybe Mummy has been to the shops and bought your brother or sister a new pair of shoes and there isn't a pair for you. Maybe your friend at school has a pencil box with lots of coloured crayons inside and you only have a few – or maybe some days everyone seems to be making a fuss of your brother or sister or friend and no one is taking any notice of you. Perhaps you feel jealous?
This is a story about a big family. The Daddy was called Jacob and he had twelve boys. Most of the boys were nearly grown up and they helped their father to look after the animals, but the two younger ones were not old enough to do that, so they helped with little jobs at home. Their names were Joseph and Benjamin. They couldn't do grown-up work, but they were good at taking messages and sometimes took picnic lunches to their big brothers in the fields. Well one day Daddy gave Joseph a very special present. It was a lovely coat with long sleeves and it had coloured stripes. Joseph was *very* pleased and put it on right away. But his big brothers were jealous. They said, 'It isn't fair; why should Joseph have a lovely new coat; he's younger than us and he doesn't work as hard as we do. Father likes him better than us. Father never gives us coats like that.' They were jealous and it made them feel cross and nasty inside.

One day when Joseph was wearing his splendid new coat his father said, 'Your big brothers are looking after the sheep. Please go and see if they are all right.' So Joseph walked up the hills and over the rocks until he saw his brothers. They saw him coming too. They still felt *very* cross and suddenly they had a very nasty idea. They thought it would be fun to pull off Joseph's new coat with the long sleeves and the bright colours and they decided to frighten him by pushing him into a big hole. That was a very nasty thought, because they felt jealous. So they pulled off his coat and pushed him into a big hole, much too deep for Joseph to climb out from. Poor Joseph. But God knew all about it and was caring for him. While they were eating their lunch the big brothers saw some men on camels riding nearer and nearer. They were men on their way to sell things in another land. The jealous brothers said, 'Let's sell Joseph to them.' They quickly pulled Joseph out of the hole and sold him to the men, who gave them twenty pieces of silver. They kept the beautiful coat and when they went home their father was very sad and thought he would never see Joseph again. But I'll tell you something special – God was looking after Joseph. He went to work for a very kind man and one day Joseph did see his father and his brothers again, because God knew all about it and took care of him every day.

Prayer   Dear God, sometimes we feel jealous of other people at home or school. Help us to be glad when other people have new things or when a lot of fuss is being made of them. Thank you that you love us and are taking care of us all the time. Amen.

Song   'God takes good care of me each day'. *Come and Sing*, Scripture Union.

14TH DAY   WILLING TO SAY SORRY

Bible story   The Prodigal Son, Luke chapter 15, verses 11–32
This story may be found in *Storytime 2*, page 53, Scripture Union.

Prayer   Lord Jesus, sometimes I do silly and naughty things. I am sorry. Please help me to say I am sorry to Mummy and Daddy when I am rude and to my friends when I am unkind. Thank you for loving me all the time. Amen.

Song   'For the things that I've done wrong'. *Come and Sing*, Scripture Union.

15TH DAY   MAKING A GOOD CHOICE

Bible story   Solomon the wise king, 1 Kings chapter 3, verses 5–14
It would be helpful if some time before telling this story the children were familiar with the book *Would you rather?* John Burningham, Jonathan Cape (to help them understand what choosing means).
If someone said, 'You can wish for anything you like and it will come true,' I wonder what you would choose? You might choose a new bike or you might want a little puppy or a special new toy. You might find it hard to choose. This is a story about a king called King Solomon. He had to choose something. One night he had a very wonderful dream. God said to him, 'You can choose anything you like and I will give it to you.' I expect King Solomon thought very hard before he made up his mind. He might have asked God for a lot of money, so he could always have his favourite things for dinner and lots of comfy chairs in his palace. He probably thought he could choose to live for a very long time, longer than anyone else. Then he might have thought he could ask God to make his country very strong, with lots of brave soldiers to win his battles. It would be nice to know he would always be safe. It was very hard to choose. Then King Solomon remembered something important. He was the king and he had a lot of people to look after in his country. Sometimes when people had arguments King Solomon had to show them the right thing to do. Sometimes when people were sad or worried he had to help them and say just the right thing to make them feel happier. Sometimes when people did naughty things he had to help them to feel sorry and put things right. King Solomon said, 'I wish I knew how to help all the people in my country. I wish I knew what to say when they need my advice, when they ask me what to do. *That's* what I'll ask God for. I'll ask him to make me very wise. I want to be a good king. Sometimes I don't know how to help everyone, so I'll ask God to show me.' So Solomon asked for wisdom and God was very pleased indeed. God said, 'You might have asked for lots of money for yourself, but you didn't. You might have asked for a long life or for your soldiers to win all the battles, but instead you asked for wisdom, so you can help all the people in your land. I am glad you were not greedy. You chose a very good thing, so I will make you wise and I will make you rich too and if you do all the things I tell you, you will live a long long time also.'
Then King Solomon woke up. Was it just a dream? Solomon found that God did make him a wise king and he said such a lot of sensible things that many of them are written in the Bible for us to read. He was able to help many people and sort out their problems. Isn't it good that King Solomon chose to help the people in his country? He didn't choose something just for himself.

Prayer   Dear God, I sometimes want a new toy or something just for me, to make *me* happy. Please remind me that it is more important to want to be good and helpful, so that other people will be happy too, for Jesus' sake. Amen.

Song   'God is pleased when we are friends'. *Come and Sing Some More*, Scripture Union.

16TH DAY   BEING GRATEFUL

Bible story   The Ten Lepers, Luke chapter 17, verses 11–19
This story may be found in *Storytime 2*, page 72, Scripture Union.
It could be followed by a discussion, encouraging the children to say what they are especially grateful for.
'Give thanks to the Lord, for he is good'. from Psalm 106.

Prayer   Ask the children to join in at the end of each line with the words 'We thank you',
Lord Jesus,
For our beautiful and interesting world – We thank you
For our families and friends – We thank you
For our food and clothes – We thank you
For our toys and books – We thank you
For our strong healthy bodies – We thank you
For your love for us all – We thank you. Amen.

Song   'This is the day'. *Come and Sing Some More*, Scripture Union.
OR   'Thank you Lord for this fine day'. *Come and Sing Some More*, Scripture Union.